LAUNDRY CAN WAIT

DOROTHY CADET

© 2010 Dorothy Cadet
All Rights Reserved.

No part of this publication may be reproduced, stored in a retrieval system, or transmitted, in any form or by any means, electronic, mechanical, photocopying, recording, or otherwise, without the written permission of the author.

First published by Dog Ear Publishing
4010 W. 86th Street, Ste H
Indianapolis, IN 46268
www.dogearpublishing.net

dog ear
PUBLISHING

ISBN: 978-160844-462-5

This book is printed on acid-free paper.

Printed in the United States of America

"Dorothy's parenting style is a perfect blend of nurturing and no-nonsense. I love her positive attitude and her ability to laugh at herself and all that raising children in these times entails. Her perspective is often inspiring, enlightening and always encouraging. Somehow she is able to balance her roles as wife, mother, and woman, and she does so with grace and no apologies. I am blessed to call her a friend." Pastor Tammy Zubeck, Professor of Mathematics, Pastor and Teacher, AZ

"Dorothy is a woman who perseveres to obtain God's best not only for herself but also for those who have been put before her by God. Life can be pretty demanding for Dorothy as a wife, mom, daughter, sister, friend, leader and servant. Dorothy's love for her husband is carried with such elegance; her passion for her children is unparalleled; and her desire to minister to the women who have chosen a journey of motherhood, is what fuels her to create a legacy of joy and victory! Her blog, on her website www.DacBooks.com is truly a reflection of her joy in being a mom. She does this by capturing every little moment and allowing God to reveal the preciousness of His children." Lina Flannagan, Finance Professional & Blogger, AZ

"Dorothy Cadet writes about the ups and downs of parenting with humor and compassion. Her advice is kind and sound and clearly based on hands-on experience. Reading *'Laundry Can Wait'* is like sitting down with a cup of coffee and a good friend – definitely a book for current and would-be parents." Sarah Bryant, novelist, Ireland

"The demands of being a mom can be overwhelming at times, and the first time I read Laundry Can Wait, I was truly blessed! There's nothing like reading stories from other moms that can make you laugh, cry, and most importantly help you feel normal; which is what Dorothy has done in her special blog on her website www.DacBooks.com!" Liz Young, Bethel World Outreach Center, Mom Builders, TN

"Dorothy, in her real, down-to-earth and wonderful way, carries a depth that relates to all moms. She is inspiring and has creative ways to make being a mom wonderful." Pastor Kelli Anderson, Founder of Daughters of Destiny, AZ

"Dorothy Cadet has an amazing gift with the written word. *Laundry Can Wait* is both inspirational and entertaining. It has in it a profound message: what's really major in the long-term? She expounds on the fact that the laundry CAN wait and many other things that innocently pull our attention from our children. In this book, Dorothy gives moms the tools to prioritizing, using the most of every opportunity, and even planning spontaneity! This is a must read for every mom, packed full of tremendous wisdom and tips." Dr. Maureen Anderson, author, co-founder Living Word Bible Church, AZ

"I love *Laundry Can Wait*.' It is warm and direct with just enough humor to make it real. I would have relished this book during my early days and later days as a mom when I felt a bit dazed and lonely. This message is as comforting as an old friend and energizing tonic. This is my new favorite gift for every new mom and dad." Susan Bryant, Bryant Educational Services, Former Boston Independent School Head and Board Member of A Better Chance, MA.

"You have a lot of great stories that demonstrate what you have learned through your life's adventures. It is clear that you have an abundance of love for your family and vice-versa. Whenever you relate one of these anecdotes in the book, the pages come alive. This book is also full of great ideas to women at all points along the road of motherhood, from beginners to 'veterans.' Between the stories and some of your one-liners, you keep the narrative voice light and enjoyable. You definitely come across as the 'every woman' you write about." Ed Red, writer, filmmaker. FL.

TABLE OF CONTENTS

Dedication vii

Forewarning ix

PART I   FOUNDATIONS

Chapter
1   WHAT DOES MY PURPOSE LOOK LIKE? 1
2   PREGNANCY REVISITED 19
3   AM I DOING THIS RIGHT? 39
4   AM I REALLY IN CONTROL? 52
5   PLAYGROUPS = ADULT CONVERSATION..............63
6   DO WHAT I SAY CHILD..73
7   CAN I SKIP WHAT YOU JUST SAID?.......................79

PART II   TAKING A MINUTE FOR YOU

8   BRING SEXY BACK (WOMAN, WIFE, MOTHER) 89
9   DAILY MENTAL HEALTH BREAKS 106
10   PHYSICAL EXERCISE – UGH! 111
11   RELATIONSHIPS AND WHY WE NEED THEM....118
12   ANNUAL "NO KIDS ALLOWED" TRIP 137
13   LOVE AND CREATE TIME FOR YOUR SPOUSE ..143

PART III LIFE'S ETERNAL MOMMY MISSION

14   BE A PLANNER WHO PLANS SPONTANEITY......163
15   FALL IN LOVE WITH BEING A MOM 170
16   LIVE FOR TODAY..180
17   TIP TIME 185

DEDICATION

I have so many people who I want to thank for not only helping me, but for being an example for me throughout this process. I first thank God for entrusting me with the care of my precious children; for giving me the burning desire to share what is presented in this book and helping me to enjoy being a mom. Next, I thank the most amazing man I have ever met, my husband, James. Not only is he my husband, he's my best friend and without his support and encouragement, I don't think I would have actually written this book. I thank my fabulous, talented, hilarious, and loving children, Victoria, Jimmy, (Olivia – departed), and Gabriella. They truly are the shining stars of my life. I now know that it was their influence, stubbornness, and laughs that helped me reach this place in my destiny. I thank my mother, Myra Simmons, as well as Pastors Maureen Anderson, Danielle Grace, Gwendolyn Ruthie Eames, Holly Anderson, Kelli Anderson, and a host of other mothers, friends and spiritual leaders.

All of you have meant so much to me and I have learned from your experiences, wisdom and guidance. It is truly a blessing to be surrounded by such great women and role models. Finally, I would like to thank Sarah Caughie who has been instrumental in helping me to focus my ideas and educating me on the life of a writer. Although a busy mom and active writer herself, she still finds time to listen, complete her own projects, and even starts new ones.

I hope all of you enjoy this labor of love and manage to see your influences upon me intertwined throughout each page.

FOREWARNING

Prepare to embark on a journey that will hopefully challenge and nudge you to become the mom that you are not only destined to become, but envision being. I have rolled out my practical experiences, both positive and negative, to highlight what I have learned during my years of motherhood and years working with adolescents and teens.

I am a mother of three wonderful children and wife of an amazing husband. I have the experience of growing up in a single-parent household with five siblings, as well as living and providing in a dual-parent household. I've experienced a financial life on public assistance through upper middle-class. I've lived in the cosmopolitan cities of New York and New Orleans, the rolling hills of Texas, and the suburbs of Arizona and Tennessee. I have worked in corporate America, been an independent contractor and real estate investor, and a stay-at-home-mom. I am a graduate of Columbia University in New York City with a degree in Psychology. I have been a teen and youth mentor for over 20 years, a Sunday school teacher, and a youth minister and teacher for over 10 years. Wow, that was a mouthful.

I not only write from my perspective as a mother, but I will draw on my experiences as a daughter, a sister, a granddaughter, a friend, a spiritual leader and one who still seeks out answers. If I draw you to a place of questions and still have not discovered an answer that is suitable for either you or me, well,...welcome to the world of uncertainty as a mom! I welcome and invite feedback, and I hope that by the end of this book, you will feel free to share your thoughts and ideas on the blog at www.DacBooks.com. I know there are many talented moms out there who can answer or post intriguing questions for all of us to ponder, or share uplifting stories of their lives as moms. I will do my best to respond to threads and posts in a timely manner...that is, after the laundry gets done, I've dropped the kids off at karate, gymnastics, or piano lessons, made dinner, fed the baby, kissed my husband, washed and folded some laundry, cleaned up the house, and grabbed a shower! Hey, you know the saying, "If you want something done, give it to a busy mom."[1]

Laundry Can Wait is all about how we as women prioritize other things that may be pressing and important over what really matters. We put others before ourselves and often times leave nothing for us to draw from. We are so busy with being moms that we might forget about the balance between being women first, wives second, and moms third. They are all important, and finding the balance is really the trick to a happy life. I don't purport to have found the answer myself. Like you, I am striving to obtain that coveted prize. I am doing better daily, and as I evolve in the nuances of my different roles, I am able to acknowledge when one of my roles is in need of attention and work hard to bring order back to that area.

As we journey together through this book, there are a few things you need to know right from the start. First and foremost, *I AM NOT A PERFECT MOM!* Nor am I the most experienced, talented, educated or organized. I make mistakes, I falter and fail, I get upset and yell at my kids and I laugh and get down on myself. My children are not perfect either. They get in trouble, make mistakes, and continually tattle. Our family is like many of yours, and I am a mom who enjoys and loves it all. There, I've said it, so now you know it and don't expect me to have all the answers to life's eternal mommy questions, no one does.

I am vulnerable, and later, you will see where I called my son the village idiot or where I yelled at my daughter for being lazy when she simply needed a ten-minute break from studying. In some of my better times, I rejoice in my "great mommy moments," as I call them, where I allowed my daughter to wear her play clothes to the store or got beat while playing video games with my five-year old son.

I wrote this book because I wanted to make someone laugh and know that as a mom, you're not alone, even when it seems like it's just you and the kids against the world. None of us are perfect, and in spite of our best efforts, we won't always get it right. It's important to know that it's OK. You are not necessarily a bad mom and more than likely will not mentally scar your child for life.

Whether your child is two and you're remembering a toothless smile, your angel is 16 and just learning to drive, or you're expecting your first grandchild, I hope you reminisce and walk down memory lane. If you're a mom-in-training, this should encourage you as you prepare for one of the most important roles you will ever fulfill.

You have the freedom to be you and enjoy your children and your motherhood. You alone were given your child because you are the perfect mom for that child. It's a daunting task at times, but it's one that is the most worthwhile and rewarding of all careers in this world.

Second, I make suggestions or tell about my own experiences or the experiences of others. Before implementing any of the information, please mull it over in your mind, think of your family's personalities and dynamics, and then use it if you can. If not, maybe it's something that needs to be tweaked for later use in your child's development.

I will mention some home remedies or other health related topics and I defer to your judgment and research. If you have specific questions regarding health issues or concerns, please consult a trained medical professional, as I am not a medical professional. None of these statements have been reviewed or evaluated by a medical professional or board, and you are advised to seek medical assistance from a licensed professional regarding anything that you read in this book or hear from anyone else.

Finally, you will find that I am opinionated, fun loving, straight talking, and view things from a common sense perspective. I believe that as moms, we need to have a plan and goal in mind so that as we raise our children, we can be proud of our accomplishments and learn from our mistakes. Even under the best of circumstances, child rearing is not all sunflowers and gumdrops, but it is worth every minute. We have to cherish ourselves, encourage one another and learn to prioritize ourselves in the midst of helping everyone else.

In essence, there is more to life than laundry. Making memories that last a lifetime is one of the most important things we can do as women. I hope that I can prompt someone to make a change that benefits her family; rejoice with someone doing everything she thinks is "right;" and let all women, wives, and moms know that you can raise the child of your dreams. Enjoy your family and love them where they are by helping them to be all that they and you have dreamed of them becoming. It all starts with growing into the person you desire to become. Even if it doesn't seem like it now, each person will find their own voice and become unique and productive within their own right.

Expect to read stories that might make you wince, laugh or even cry. You will read stories of practical wisdom from not only my experiences, but also the experience of hundreds of women, and even some men that I know and respect.

Some of what you will not find in this book is a heavy emphasis on direct scriptural or Biblical quotes. I am a practical Christian author who loves God with all my heart and soul. I endeavor to live my life as an example of what is taught in the Bible. The lessons and ideas expounded on in the Bible will be expressed in real-life application, along with a host of other sources and quotes.

This book will not necessarily be for everyone, but it is my desire that as we experience this journey, we live it on purpose and with a passion.

Now that you know a little bit about me and the purpose of this book, let's get to the fun stuff and enjoy being the best mom in the whole wide world, even if you may not know it yet! From this point forward, we are friends, and I hope you will treat this book as a conversation between friends. Highlight passages or write in the notes section if something jumps out at you. Talk back when I make a good point. Feel free to smile or cry when I share my stories and life. Now, grab a comfy place where you can read, sit back, have a cup of tea, cocoa, cup of "joe" or whatever it is you drink, and let's go!

I, Dorothy Cadet, dub thee reader,

THE BEST MOM IN THE WORLD!

So, now you can walk in your royal garment, aka bathrobe, and yell to one of your children, "Child, the Queen needs her royal slippers and a glass of milk, please. Quickly child you mustn't keep royalty waiting!"

CHAPTER 1

WHAT DOES MY PURPOSE LOOK LIKE?

"I know God will not give me anything I can't handle. I just wish that He didn't trust me so much."
— Mother Theresa

By beginning to define what our purpose looks like, we are laying the foundation of successful motherhood. As moms, we are getting a jump-start by defining our purpose and setting goals. We will be able to think of how each of our children is different and how, as moms, we respond to various situations. With this in mind, we can take that information and clarify our parenting philosophy.

Many of us get involved in things without a clear picture or vision of what we hope to accomplish. We know that when we play a game, our goal is to win. However, sometimes the how-to gets murky and we don't have a clear plan. Now, I know there are different personality types: some gravitate to "flying by the seat of their pants" while some are "scheduled down to the second." There are also many people that fall in the middle or mix the two. Whatever your personality type, consider creating a vision of what you want to see accomplished in your role as a woman, wife and mother.

After James and I got married and he was about to discharge from the Army as a Captain of military intelligence, we needed a clearly detailed plan of how we would support ourselves. We lived in Killeen, Texas, a small town outside of Austin that was economically stagnant and did not have much room for professional growth. I was a real estate agent whose commissions were not dependable, and he was about to lose his steady salary. Our plan was to locate, purchase and close on real estate investments that only required a minimum of 50% occupancy to pay the mortgage note, and over 50% occupancy would be our income. Once we located, purchased and closed, the properties were all 75%-100% occupied, yielding us a steady monthly profit. Because this was my career field and James desired to focus on finances, we made a natural transition and built upon our existing expertise. We did not take a blind stab in the dark, but instead, made sure we would be able to support ourselves.

Let's take this book as another example. I didn't wake up one morning and say, "Hey, I think I'll write a book today. Let me flow and see what comes out!" OK, well, maybe on some days I did that. However, I had a carefully crafted outline of topics with a clear beginning, middle, end and defined sections in between. I knew where I wanted to go from the moment I started typing.

You may want to create a similar type of outline of how you want to proceed with your life as a mom. Start out with a rough draft and then write down the most important things that you desire to accomplish. As you create more time for yourself, flesh it out and then start writing and living out the masterpiece of your life. It does not have to be done all in one day. Consider it a work in progress, but don't let it take years. I know I sound like a 9th grade English teacher, but I have to go with what works.

I recently came across an interesting article about goals and what stops people from attaining their goals. According to Douglas Vermeeren's article entitled *"Why People Fail to Achieve Their Goals,"*[2] only about 20% of the population set goals and only 30% of those goal-setters ever achieve their goals. His article lists 10 reasons why (explanations are paraphrased):

1. *Fear of success and/or failure* – You don't bother attempting to attain a goal because you fear it is a lose-lose situation or you are looked down upon because of a lack of belief in self or potential.
2. *Lack of understanding about the goal-setting process* - You view it as a one shot deal to be checked off and not a process to change you for a long-term benefit.
3. *Lack of commitment to the goal* - You have to give it your all to get results. Many are not willing to completely dedicate themselves.
4. *Inactivity* – Some people write things down but never take action. You have to start the steps now to achieve the results you have written down.
5. *Analysis paralysis* – Many people let questions and doubts paralyze them from starting until they have all the answers to "what if." You'll never have all the answers, so make decisions based on the future, considering the now.
6. *Lack of a real destination* – You have to know where you

want to go in order to know when you get there. Visualize and be able to describe it so that it becomes something attainable and concrete.
7. *Failing to plan* – You have a goal but don't understand how to achieve the goal. You have to learn to use your resources and relationships to help you in the process.
8. *Having too many goals* – Achieve one goal at a time because if you go in many directions, you will eventually end up with nothing accomplished. Once you achieve one goal, then begin the process for the next and ensuing goals.
9. *Feeling Unworthy of the end result* – Don't sabotage yourself because you feel like you don't deserve the goal. Have confidence you can achieve.
10. *Lack of motivation to change* – When you are satisfied with what and where you are in life, you remain stagnant. Change and goal attainment only happen when you're ready to break the status quo and truly want something better in life.

Mr. Vermeeren also states that in writing goals, you have to understand the difference between "being" (who you want to be) and "doing" (what you want to achieve). These two areas will span across four categories: wealth, health, relationships, and self-fulfillment. Achieving balance and success in each area requires both the "being" and "doing" part of each category.

To set goals and outline your role as a mom, start by carefully looking at and identifying what you imagine your purpose to be as a mother.

As a new mom raising my first child, my purposes, or rather goals, were to make sure not to drop Victoria, feed and change her in a timely manner and remember that I couldn't go anywhere without her or leave her by accident. I also set a goal of making sure to get a shower at least every two days. If I did these things, I felt complete success.

The second time around with my son, Jimmy, my primary goal was to assure Victoria we loved her, even though Jimmy was now the baby. Another was to make sure he didn't whiz on me when I changed his diaper. The last was to make sure I showered daily and learned how to get my schedule under control.

With my third child, Gabriella, my main objectives were to stop her from drinking the bath water and eating too much paper or dirt when we went to the park. I also set a priority to get pictures of her drinking the bath water, eating paper and dirt so I could tease her when she got older.

So you see, with the progression of children came different priorities. I joked about some, but hey, that's all I had at the time. I didn't have insight into the importance of living in the moment while parenting with the end in mind. That way, I didn't major on the minors. I realized that I had a *job* as a parent, not simply a *role* as a parent.

In applying Mr. Vermeeren's list to my original ideas, I would say that I only had a commitment to attaining my goals. All I knew or cared about was what I didn't want to do as a new mom. I had no tangible picture in my mind or written down, of what I wanted for the future. I lived day-to-day and parented that way. I was living out my *role* because I didn't understand the concept of my *job* as a parent.

In my opinion, the difference between my *job* versus my *role* as a parent is best explained as this: my *job* entails work and tough choices, whereas my *role* is principle centered and involves my presence and nurturing. In my *job*, I have to actively make choices that steer my children in the right direction. My *job* requires that I place my long-term goals for my children ahead of circumstances that arise to test my convictions on a particular subject. In my *role*, I am my children's cheerleader and confidant. My *role* as a parent leads, guides, directs and gives them that warm, fuzzy feeling. My *role* continually reinforces my unwavering love and support for my children. There are times that I struggle with the delineations, but the more I become aware of the situations and what each demands, I learn to respond correctly.

When Victoria wanted to spend the night at a new friend's house, she was not permitted. A rule we have in our home is that we must meet the parents and friends a few times before allowing our child to spend the night at their friend's house. My *role* said to let her go and have fun at the sleepover. My *job* said that I should not compromise or bend the rules for the safety of my daughter. It was not a popular decision, but eventually, we got to know the parents and child; Victoria was allowed to sleep over at her friend's house, and her friend was allowed to sleep over our house.

WHAT DID BEING A MOM REALLY LOOK LIKE FOR ME?

I remember being asked in high school what I wanted to do with my life when I graduated. I often said either a psychiatrist or a business tycoon. Being a stay-at-home-mom was not in the top five things I envisioned for my life. My life goals began with going to college, majoring in psychology at Columbia University, learning what people thought and analyzing the motives for their actions. It was in college that I discovered I enjoyed psychology, but I relished business more. After graduating from college, I entered corporate America and was on my way to achieving my dreams and becoming a thriving member of the professional community. I worked in corporate America for just over four years.

In my fifth year, I met my husband James during a meeting for independent business owners. I was smitten by him and decided I was done with being a city dweller, and I wanted more from life (more on this in a later chapter). I was always stressed, felt rushed, and I saw the effects of continual tension in the lives of my co-workers. I was more than ready for a life and career change. I subsequently moved to Texas from New York and became a salesperson. I started with telecommunications, then security systems, and settled on real estate. I discovered I had a knack for helping and teaching people.

Eighteen months after my move to Texas, James and I got married. Within two years, I became pregnant with our daughter, Victoria. Because we had our own business, I had the luxury of bringing Victoria into the office daily. However, after nine months, I could no longer sufficiently monitor her while taking care of our real estate and property management workload. We made the decision to put Victoria in daycare so that we could focus on the business and comfortably support our family of three. I continued running our business for nearly two years before becoming pregnant with our son Jimmy. It was at that point we felt the financial strain of paying for one infant in daycare, plus an office space, staff salary, and all the expenses of our own household. It was becoming difficult to sustain it all, and we made the very difficult decision to reduce our expenses by closing our office location and raising both of the children at home. We made the tough decision to close and move the office to our home. I was afforded more flexibility by working real estate by appointment only.

After three months of conducting business from home, it became too demanding to keep a two-year-old and an infant entertained while taking business calls and setting up real estate appointments. I had to call it quits. We sold the property management and leasing business to a fellow realtor, and I deactivated my real estate license.

There may be many women caught between staying home with their children and going to work. Sometimes, it is a situation where staying at home is not possible and both you and your spouse have to work. My husband and I have been faced with the above situations and it was not easy. I hated the thought of leaving my kids and returning to the work force. At the same time, we had to keep a roof over our heads, the lights on, and food on the table. If you are in this situation, I suggest you weigh all of your options and revisit Mr. Vermeeren's point five. Make your decisions for the future, considering the now. As my friend Tammy says, "I can do anything if I know it has a definite purpose and an end." Sometimes the purpose may be to work now so you can stay home later.

I will attest to understanding what the choices look like and how the situation feels. Initially, we debated my continuing to work, but ultimately decided my staying at home was best. We streamlined our finances by reducing our expenses and setting a very tight budget. I know what it is like to have to raise a family of four on an income of $30,000! We chose: to cut coupons, only having basic cable, using our cell phones for long distance calls, and learning how to re-purpose leftovers instead of eating out. We didn't have a ton of creature comforts, but we were fine with that. As long as we had our basic needs met, we were able to enjoy and live life contentedly.

Later, when James' salary increased, we added back in some of those things, but in moderation. We worked to spend and live either below or within our means. Our mindset mainly focused on making sure we had a safe, comfortable place to live, lights, water and food. If we had those basic needs met, everything above that was "gravy." Don't get me wrong, we like the better things in life too; we just knew that when we were on a strict budget, some things needed to be cut out.

Having abruptly made the choice to streamline our finances and raise our children at home, I found myself with two small children and flat out of ideas and know-how. I didn't know what to do with two small children at home all day, every day. I was unsure whether I should let them play all day and then watch a little television to round things out. I didn't know if they were able to do arts and crafts, or if I would have the patience to allow them to "discover" their creative abilities. I wanted them to go outside and play, but being a native New Yorker, I felt like the Texas woods was not a safe place for small children. I had no earthly idea what to do, and I was getting bored. I kept thinking that when I was young, all I did was watch television and play all day. I turned out fine, so why was this such a struggle?

I decided to take a childcare class to learn what the daycares taught the kids so I could make use of my time. I even bought books on how to run and operate a daycare. I wasn't planning on running that kind of business, but I needed to find something to occupy my time, my mind and help teach the kids something during the day.

My efforts to learn what they did in a daycare didn't seem to go past a "good idea." I reviewed and skimmed the books and then they sat on the shelf collecting dust. It hit me hard when I realized that my baby girl was three-years-old and my baby boy was one-year-old and I had nothing to show for our time other than a few pictures. I let so many precious moments pass. I can never get back a toothless smile or even a bear hug or a full guttural laugh. I missed out on silly art projects and sing-a-longs because I was self-absorbed and focused on my lack of knowledge. I didn't use the resources around me to help me grow into my role as a mom.

Because we lived in a rural area of Texas, there were no parks near our house. We had to drive ten miles into town in order for the kids to get out and play freely with other children. One day while sitting at the park, I listened to a dad talk about how miserable he was because he had to stay home with his son that day and how bored he was watching television. I heard several moms also talk about how they could tell you every kid show and channel. I couldn't help but chime in and agree with their sentiments. I was bored with watching television and doing very little during our day.

It was at that moment that I realized I was wasting both my and my children's time. I didn't do anything that challenged them or me. I thought of the countless months I spent in real estate classes learning how to be a real estate professional or the years I spent in the classes on the executive retail track. I spent so much time achieving professional success, but I did not give a wholehearted effort at studying and training to be a mom. It dawned on me that I had to learn to make everything produce! It took a little while for the theory of everything producing to settle in my mind. However the picture became very clear.

Making everything produce is an idea that says, "I won't be wasteful." I won't waste time, talents or treasures. Time is the greatest non-renewable resource in our lives as it encompasses our memories; I won't waste time allowing my children or myself to watch television programs that do not teach or force our minds to work. Talents are the things that we possess such as mental, emotional, or physical abilities; I will not allow my children to give up on a sport, instrument, or educational opportunity because it seems difficult. Treasures are the things such as our money or investments; I will not allow my children or myself to throw away or spend money without understanding value or budgeting. When we hold our time, talents, and treasures in high regard, we won't waste them.

We have to recognize and value these resources. When we think of making our children and our possessions productive, we must figure out how to best capitalize upon what is exhibited.

Because Victoria loved to sing, we would often make up songs. I would give her different items, and she would create a whole song about them.

Jimmy loved to play, so I made up a game in which I put things out of order and he put them back in the original order. We fostered creativity as well as memory recall, all while playing and being entertained.

In order not to waste the money I had spent on childcare books and supplies the previous year, I finally read them and began using them daily. I was challenged how to teach at age-appropriate levels so I was being productive as well. I made our time together both fun and productive. I am so glad I did because we all learned a lot and benefitted.

COO of PERSONNEL DEVELOPMENT AND OPERATIONS

It's funny how when someone asks any stay-at-home-mom what she does, she'll have to sum up 10 different job descriptions into one succinct job title. My title is "Chief Operating Officer of Personnel Development and Operations." What does that mean?

I am the primary person in charge of making sure that the children are well adjusted, respectful, healthy, sociable, mentally and physically stimulated daily, and capable of making good sound choices and judgment. All of this while maintaining the household: clean house, meals prepared, children's jungle gym and playmate, nurse, teacher, chauffeur, etc.

Now, add those wifely duties. If you're single, add the hefty chore of going to work daily with no help at home. It's a hard and heavy task at times. All of you moms-in-training thought you had a hard job! However, what some may see as a burden, I now call my joy.

I used to view it as a burden because I didn't understand the intent. Once I changed my mindset and realized that I was the COO of Personnel Development and Operations, my tune changed. I began to run my house like I would a business. I began to schedule my days (task-oriented for the children and time-oriented for my own sanity). I took a special interest in instilling in the children how to be responsible for their own choices and how to solve problems. Yes, they were two and three at the time, but they weren't too young to understand these things (once I explained it in their language, of course.) I saw the benefits of having helped them understand responsibility and I expect to continue seeing the fruit of it as they continue to grow older.

I introduced the completion of household chores as a learning tool for both them and me. It was a struggle at first. Matching socks by color, texture, length and type was hard. Over the years, it has become easier, and they can do that task by themselves. While cleaning up, we sorted toys by type, features and the like. When I made meals, I got their help (to a certain extent) and, during weekly meal planning, we wrote out our meal schedule a week ahead so that I wouldn't rush around at the last minute. By getting their help, I believe I birthed in them the love and joy of cooking.

I enrolled the children in learning about life and working around the house so that they would take ownership of their roles, and learn the basic skills needed by independent adults. I am sure we all know at least a handful of adults who never learned how to cook, do their own laundry, or even clean up after themselves. My goal is to assist my children by equipping them with all the skills they will need as they mature. These skills later became helpful during our times of transitioning from one city to another.

TRANSITIONS

After moving from Texas to Arizona, I interviewed for several different jobs without receiving an offer. My motivation was to help make the transition from a moderately struggling income level to a more comfortable income level, plus I wanted to get back to working outside of the home. I thought my job as the COO of Personnel Development and Operations had been successful and we had all learned a lot and bonded. I thought I had been faithful over what God had put me in charge of and now I was going to be promoted back into the business world. After not receiving a job offer, despite follow-up interviews, those hopes were all but smashed to pieces. I had to focus on making my position as a stay-at-home-mom work. Thankfully, James received a job promotion and raise. Our new income was enough to help us meet the higher cost of living we encountered after moving to Arizona.

Even though I enjoyed being at home daily with my children, a part of me was bitter and resentful. The honest truth behind it all was that I felt like my life was wasting away. I hated that I was an Ivy-League College graduate and I had been reduced to taking care of children and doing laundry all day. I love a clean house just like the next gal, but I was SO NOT the domestic diva type, and it was eating me up inside. I loved thinking of my home as a business and me the COO of Personnel Development and Operations, but I honestly thought that position was temporary and only meant to last for a year or two. Remember, stay-at-home-mom was not on my list of top five things to do with my life.

I even began to hate meeting my husband's co-workers. The look I would receive from them when I told them I stayed at home seemed to automatically discount and unconsciously assume I was not educated or able to have an "adult" conversation. That drove me absolutely nuts because I wanted and needed that affirmation and conversation. I would often binge on junk foods to fill the emptiness and numb the feeling that my life was in a total tailspin and I had no control over anything in it.

I wanted to go and get a job, but I hated the idea of punching a clock. It had been five years since I had worked for a company with a supervisor and I was none too eager to do that again. The entrepreneurial spirit burned inside of me and I could not resist its allure, yet I needed the freedom and challenge it provided. Motherhood was certainly not a breeze, quite the contrary, but it felt like I was operating on autopilot.

I knew that each day of the week was associated with a different household task. I did the laundry, went grocery shopping, made sure dinner was prepared by 6pm, cleaned the bathrooms, swept the floors, and made sure the kids did something, anything productive, even if it was coloring. I was doing everything to keep myself busy and produce what I deemed as "happiness," but all I felt was empty and unfulfilled. Oddly enough, it was during one of the job interviews that I was asked about my three-, five-, and ten-year life plan. I drew a blank and it hit me that I didn't have a plan or an idea of what I wanted to do with my life.

Sorry that this part is not all bubbles and sugarplums. I don't think I'm the only one out there who has felt this way. I know there is some mom wondering whether she made a mistake leaving the corporate world to stay home with her children. How about the mom who is single and working to make ends meet or even has the bases covered but wishes she could leave the work world and spend time with her precious child? How about the woman who wants to become pregnant and is not sure if this is the right time to start a family? I can go through a multitude of situations and scenarios. The bottom line is, we all want to know what being a mom is like and can we do it differently or perfect what we have.

Truthfully ladies, the best answer to this question can only be answered by YOU. There are many lenses that each of us looks through and has to deal with life through. What works for me may not work for you. You have to figure out if leaving the workforce is economically viable for your family. You have to make tough decisions on decreasing or eliminating items from your monthly budget. There are many things to consider. Just be prepared on all fronts so you can make an informed decision you can live with.

During my transition periods, there were many things that I learned and continue to practice. I have found that it helps to befriend at least three or four other women with children so that we each took turns babysitting one another's children. This helps each mom build a core group of friends with whom to have a few "exhale" moments. We'll discuss this more in the playgroup section.

You have to make time during the day, whether it is 15 minutes or two hours, to relax and pour back into you. You need to create time to do some sort of physical activity. It can be yoga, Pilates, kickboxing, spin, dance, stretch, walking, running, or whatever. Just do something. You will be happier, more relaxed, and able to handle life's challenges more appropriately.

Some women find a hobby. I know, when you're busy, how do you find time for a hobby? You make it. For me, it was writing. Find something that keeps you mentally stimulated and pushing forward.

Just a clarification, each of these things don't have to be done during separate times. As women, we know how to multi-task.

There's nothing that says you can't take a hot bath, relax, and read for 30 minutes before bed. What about doing some form of exercise with a group of friends? That way you spend time with friends, are accountable to someone else and do something for yourself. I have to borrow Nike's slogan and say, "Just Do It." Do something for you so you can be a better woman, wife to your hubby, or mom to your children.

WRITE THE VISION

While in Arizona at a business conference, James met a wonderful woman by the name of Allyson Lewis. She's a very successful financial advisor, author, mother and speaker. After a mutual speaking event, he brought home a book that would change my thinking as well as my life. Mrs. Lewis' book, *The Seven Minute Difference: Small Steps to Big Changes*[3] taught me the importance of not only writing down my goals, but performing small things daily to effect a big change later. Her book challenged me to take seven to fifteen minutes per day to make a small step toward a major life goal. As I applied the basic principles to my life, I became a real COO of Personnel Development and Operations uniquely qualified to reap the same benefits as any Fortune 500 executive. Because of the foundations learned, you will see my list below of the vision I have written for my life.

It is important to get into the habit of writing your thoughts and vision for your and your children's future. This is a simple and powerful concept once you grab a hold of it. It is said that the top 3% of the most successful people in the world have written out and recite daily their lifetime achievement goals. To get you started on the road to setting mom-based goals, I offer the following ideas. If you are a mom-in-training, even before you become pregnant, write how you envision your pregnancy, labor and delivery to happen. The idea is to think positive and allow your words to create your environment. This is not a promise, just a way to get your mind focused on the bigger picture. For all moms, what characteristics would you love to see develop in your children? Express the grades you desire for them to receive in school, their friends' and future spouse's characteristics. Write down the legacy you want to create for your family.

When you're all done crafting the plan you foresee for your children, begin composing what you hope to have accomplished as a mother. What are some of life's lessons you hope to have taught your children? What type of woman do you imagine yourself to be? Write down the type of relationship you hope to have with your children and the example by which you desire to lead. Lastly, imagine what you hope your children will say about you when they are adults.

My list looks like this:

1. During pregnancy, I hope to have safe, enjoyable pregnancies free of any major issues, medical problems or severe morning sickness.
2. I want to have my labor and delivery last less than eight hours combined.
3. I want to see my children grow up to be strong men and women who not only make good decisions, but who internally know what the right thing to do is and make the conscious decision to do it. I want my children to be leaders who set good examples and only follow those people who can make them better people.
4. I want my children to get the best grades they can possibly get by applying themselves fully to the goal of doing well. I desire them to get A's and B's, but will focus on them striving to always do their best. I will do all within my power to help them study, learn and maintain excellence in what they do.
5. I pray their friends have positive characters and moral upbringing. I pray that their friends only want to help and never purposely hurt my children. I hope and pray no one who has ill will, is negative, abusive, or has low morals or character will befriend my children.
6. I pray that my children's spouses are filled with the love of Jesus Christ and love my children unconditionally. I hope that their spouses treat and esteem them always, and that their relationships have Christ as the center.
7. I hope to leave a legacy of marital unity that is filled with honor and the love of Christ that my children, grandchildren, and great grandchildren can exemplify.
8. I hope to look back on my life and see the love, joys, and memories that were established and created.
9. I hope that I have taught my children how to love God, be good decision makers, respectful of others, good communicators, have a strong personal and moral character, and how to be productive members of society.

10. I imagine myself to be a teacher who is not prideful, but is ever learning. I see myself as sexy, lively, fun-loving, caring, compassionate, honest, and dedicated.
11. I hope my children see in me, humility, strength, determination and excellence. I hope they see me as not afraid to show love or apologize when I am wrong. I hope they see me lead as well as follow, while being diligent in the process.
12. I hope, that as my children grow up, we have an amazing relationship and they see me as a loving mother, a great resource, someone who's opinion matters because of respect, and they willfully want to spend time with me. I hope they say that they had the best mother in the whole wide world.

That is my list, but you should make your own. Initially, it may be a tall order and one that will take some forethought. Heck, my list took me six months to create, and I update it regularly. Your vision is something that will change over time as it becomes clearer to you. The goal is to get you thinking and moving in the direction of being a great mom on purpose and not by chance. You will never be able to hit a target that you cannot clearly see. Learn to see the target, and then continue to take aim at it until you finally believe that you will consistently land on the bull's eye.

Outlining our vision or goals is something we are familiar with, but may have fallen away from practicing. When we were in school and had to write English papers, we created an outline. We researched to find facts, graphs, and supporting documentation. We did it in school for a grade; why not apply that type of dedication, research, and vision to the most important task we will ever undertake: the role of being a mom?

IS LAUNDRY YOUR PRIORITY?

What's more important to you right now, spending time with your children and making memories that will stick in everyone's heart forever, or making sure that load of colored clothes gets washed, dried, ironed and put away? Laundry can wait!

Is it more important to share a tender moment with your spouse, or spend an extra 30 minutes getting ahead of your to-do list? Laundry can wait!

Is it more important to refresh yourself with exercise, have a calming moment over a cup of tea, read a book, take a nap, or even just have some 'alone time', or make sure that you get that sink scrubbed out? Laundry can wait!

Is it more important to maintain or even start a friendship, or make excuses about being shy? Laundry can wait!

In essence, in the midst of living your daily lives, don't make laundry a priority! Laundry is any and everything that keeps you from fulfilling your life's purpose and growing the relationships that are most important to you. As with physical laundry, the concept really encapsulates the idea that this thing will still be there, and even when you get it done, it will need to be done again. Laundry is so much deeper than the basic notion of dirty clothes. Don't let your mind stop there. You have to learn to be smart with your time and selective with how and what you choose to do.

As a stay-at-home-mom, my laundry really is laundry. I just can't fathom how a family of five-plus consistently has seven-plus loads of laundry EVERY WEEK! Not half loads, but baskets bursting to overflowing loads. It just blows my mind how many clothes we go through. My "laundry" is also procrastination and being a perfectionist. Well, I used to be a perfectionist. I have since given that up and turned to a more relaxed version. My angst is that if I know I can't fully complete something, then I don't start because it would bother me to have things lingering. So, even though I love my house to be clean, I know that if my toddler is playing I wait until her nap or bedtime to straighten things and put them away. Better yet, she and I have started singing the "clean up song." Come on moms. Sing it with me!

Clean up, clean up, everybody everywhere, clean up.
It's time for (insert child's name) to clean up, her toys, put this here, put this there, and clean up.

This is our rendition and make it work based on the day. However, I have learned that sometimes, the toys are going to have to stay out and I am now fine with that. It was a process to get here, but I had to learn to do what worked with our family.

One past Thanksgiving, our family spent time with my husband's side of the family. We had such a great time, and we learned something interesting. Our children didn't know how to play video games. It's just not something I really gravitate towards unless it teaches something. Some may think, "Hooray," while others may think, "those poor kids." We felt bad and, because James absolutely loves video games, we caved in and bought a game system. It really was a great investment because I learned that Victoria loves to play sports-related games whereas Jimmy loves to play karate and driving games. They're both really good at them, but I, on the other hand, need some major help.

One day in the midst of cleaning the house, Jimmy kept jumping around to get my attention with how well he was scoring on the driving game.

"OK Jimmy, that's nice," was my response.

"Mom, don't you want to see? Come and take a look!"

"OK, honey, give me a few minutes to clean off the table and sweep the floor."

"But mom, you have to see this. I'm beating the computer. I'm the best!"

It was at that moment I realized a window of opportunity had opened up: my son was inviting me to join his world. He wanted me to take a break from my cleaning (aka *laundry*) and spend some time with him. I immediately stopped what I was doing and sat next to him and watched him play his video game. Even though I was not really into the game system, I asked him to teach me how to do it. His eyes lit up and he was so happy to show me how to play his driving game. He still references that time by laughing and telling everyone how he beat mommy at driving.

This was one of my proud mommy moments. I got a chance to experience my child's happiness and create a memory that we cherish. Sometimes, simply speaking "to" your child and saying, "I love you" is secondary (though that is extremely important and needs to be done). It's often crucial to demonstrate your love by stopping what you deem necessary, by getting involved with the MORE IMPORTANT!

The making of memories is essential. It is that little opening of a window in the form of an invitation that allows us to peek into our children's world, to reassure them of who they are and how we see them. It is also important to ascertain how your child best communicates love and how they receive it. Some children want to be around or near you. Others want to hear you speak positive and affirming words. Some children want gifts (regardless of monetary value). Children need to know you thought of them. They want you to hug them. Some children want you to help them do things that they need to get done, such as homework.

Sometimes it's a combination of these areas, and sometimes one type will stick out more often than others. However, when you learn to communicate with your child, you will discover more of those "open windows" and the bridge to a secure foundational relationship is within reach. If you want to learn more on these categorizations, you should read, *The Five Love Languages* by Gary Chapman.[4] It is very insightful and teaches us to understand how others (adults, teens and children) view and receive love.

This is an important component because in order to understand how to make your children a priority over *laundry*, you have to value the communication and love between you. I mentioned earlier that we have to learn to parent with the end in mind. Parenting should involve the overriding themes of: making memories; instilling great qualities in our children that will last a lifetime; crafting people whom we hope will eventually want to be around us as parents, not because they have an obligation, but because they want to; and establishing morals, values and traditions, that can be passed on from generation to generation.

Learn to make your family and friends your priority and not your *laundry*. It's easy to get caught up in daily life, but there will come a point where you will want more. However, will you have laid the foundation for what you desired, or will you have to go back and create it?

"Strong Lives are motivated by dynamic purposes."
– Kenneth Hildebrand

NOTES:

Chapter 2

Pregnancy Revisited

"Life is tough enough without having someone kick you from the inside."

– Rita Rudner

You now have a better idea of how important it is to write down a vision for your life as a mom and how you have to prioritize yourself in the midst. In looking through the next few pages and reading about my pregnancy stories, you will see that I had no real vision or plan. I wish I did, but the truth is I was just winging it until I was taught differently.

For specific answers to your questions, head to your local library, favorite bookstore or internet site. There are many resources available on every topic related to pregnancy. Whether you have a pain in your side or some weird sensation, you can find answers to just about any question on a number of blog sites, mommy forums, and medical sites. There are several best-selling books that detail every stage and question you have never considered. *What to Expect When You're Expecting* by Heidi Murkoff and Sharon Mazel[5] or *The Baby Book: Everything You Need to know About Your Baby from Birth to Age Two* by William & Martha Sears, Robert Sears, and James Sears[6] are also excellent resources (see chapter 17 for additional options).

If that isn't enough, just let any mom, grandmother, friend or perfect stranger even think that you are pregnant, and immediately, you will receive more information than you can digest.

For instance, when I was pregnant with my first child Victoria, I was in a grocery store waiting in the check out line. A lady with her toddler approached me and asked the normal questions: "When are you due? Do you know the gender? Have you picked out a name?" After politely answering all her questions, she went into a dissertation of how, with her first child, she was in 22 hours of "hard" labor, without an epidural, and she had such a terrible time and it was the worst thing ever, but it all got better once she delivered her 10 pound 6 ounce baby boy. Of course that ruined my little day. I was already nervous, but she made it worse. I never even considered the prospect of delivering the equivalent of a small turkey!

After hearing this, I was reminded of something my friend Nicole told me a few years earlier: "When you hear the tough stories, just smile and listen politely, but in the back of your mind, continue to think of your pregnancy as short, pleasant, smooth and without problems. This does not deny the fact that there are many women who endure quite a lot during pregnancy and even during their labor and delivery. However, focus on pleasant thoughts and if something should change, be informed, think about what's best for the baby, and don't panic."

I heard what she said, but because I was not even married or thinking about having children at that time, it went into my mental file for later use. I thought this was good advice, as her entire labor and delivery with her first child lasted six hours, and her second child lasted five. She was the most pleasant pregnant woman I had ever met, and she enjoyed being pregnant, if there ever were a crazier idea. I took her advice to heart and I kept thinking about Nicole and how she made being pregnant look like fun and not as terrible as I had always heard about or envisioned.

Another piece of sound advice I received as a mom-in-training was from Pastor Danielle Grace. She pulled me aside and shared this nugget of wisdom: "Don't eat any and everything. In the early goings, you only need the equivalent of an extra piece of fruit. Later on, just make meals healthy and keep the snacks healthy." Pastor Danielle was a perfectly fit size six after both her children. Another woman I knew had eight children and stayed a size six based on this advice. I remember being told many times before that I could eat whatever I wanted during pregnancy. I felt betrayed that I wouldn't be able to gorge whenever I wanted without repercussions. However, I'm glad I found out the truth early and didn't completely go overboard.

All the advice was good information while pregnant, but I put it on the mental shelf while I was single, then married, without children.

VICTORIA'S STORY

I remember the day I found out I was pregnant with Victoria. I was shocked and in denial. We had lots going on and I didn't know how it was all going to work. My husband was getting out of the

Army, and he and I were about to become independent contractors. We were about to step into the world of real estate investments and entrepreneurship. It was scary and uncertain, but we had a rock solid plan and had laid the groundwork for bringing in finances to support us. I would remain a real estate agent doing all the property management work, while he took on the role of property scout and financial manager.

With our transition plan from military to civilian life in place, James and I went about planning the romantic celebration of our first anniversary. We were going to Spain to see the sights and enjoy the beauty of the land and all the Spanish culture had in store for us. The best thing about Spain was that we went round trip for a mere $40 each. (He was still in the Army, of course.) GO ARMY and flight HOPS, Hoorah! We had a great time, that is, besides the moments of daily bickering, my testiness, unseasonably cold weather, and the ten-hour return flight with no windows in the belly of an Army plane. James admits that he knew something wasn't quite right. I seemed a bit more irritable and emotional than normal.

After a wonderful week in Spain, we returned to the U.S. to begin our new journey of being unemployed, or as we called it, "Entrepreneurs." James had two final weeks before finally discharging from the Army. We decided to get our last physical exams as we weren't sure when we would get health coverage as independent contractors. I went to the doctor and they ran a battery of tests, one of which was a pregnancy test (I had no clue about that one). Now, to be clear, I was not one of those women who, like clockwork, knew when Mother Nature was going to visit. Nope, I was in that very crazy category of those who got visited whenever the feeling hit old Mother Nature!

So, in walked the doctor and said, "I know why you haven't been regular." This was very welcome news, and I thought that some great medical mystery had been solved. I would finally find out why, after at least five years, I was not regular and predictable.

I smiled, looked up, and said, "Yes."

With a huge grin, he and his assistant smiled and said, "Congratulations, you're pregnant and going to be a mom in about six months."

I was taken aback and immediately blurted out, "Well, you're wrong. I need you to run those tests again." I honestly think I stunned him more than he stunned me.

"Well, ma'am, our blood and urine tests are pretty accurate, but if you really want to, I can run them again."

"Never mind." I was completely shocked and a feeling of bewilderment came over me. However, before I walked out of the room, the magnitude of the news really hit me and I asked him, "Am I really going to be a mom?"

He smiled gently and said, "Yes, you sure are. Hope you're ready." I kept wondering how to tell James that we were pregnant. (Yes, I said, "We" because it was completely his fault.)

I wasn't ready to be a mom. We had no health coverage. Despite our best efforts to get health coverage, I had what was deemed by the insurance companies as a "pre-existing condition" for which none of the insurance companies would extend me insurance. We were out of ideas and the situation was becoming desperate. I asked several of my friends, and one finally suggested that I apply for Medicaid.

I talked it over with James and we agreed that it was important for me to maintain my health and the health of our baby with regular checkups. I applied and initially was denied and told to reapply in 30 days. James was still considered employed because he received wages higher than the median income allowed for that program cycle. I waited for 30 days, then reapplied and was accepted. It was humbling, because despite having a business and James' rank as Captain in the Army, we couldn't get health coverage. I was grateful for my experience with Medicaid and the counselor I had been assigned. For all the many benefits I received from Medicaid, I was most appreciative of their coverage of Victoria for 12 months after her birth.

Even though I read many pregnancy books, I wasn't prepared to be ultra tired from developing anemia, nor was I prepared for the aches, pains, strains, and pulling that went on in my body. I wasn't prepared for my obstetrician to tell me that he would induce me nearly two weeks early because my legs were swelling. Miss Victoria must have panicked because she decided to be delivered the very next day. I wasn't prepared to change my birthing plan of not receiving an epidural or other medications during labor. I decided to get an epidural for the immense pain. I wasn't prepared for eight hours of labor and delivery when Victoria got stuck for three of those eight hours. I pushed so hard during labor that my eyes swelled and I looked more like a boxer than a new mom with that mommy-glow. After all of this, Princess Victoria weighed 6 pounds 15½ ounces and was 20 inches long.

Laundry Can Wait

In the midst of delivering Victoria, something both amusing, and surprising happened. In the fifth hour of active labor, we all thought she was about to crown and we'd be able to eat lunch. All around the delivery room, everyone put in lunch orders. James and I put ours in, and then the nurse who was helping me push on the other side of James pulled out her five dollars and put it in her shirt pocket. "Push Mrs. Cadet" is all I kept hearing from her. Finally, after pushing for three additional hours, Victoria came out. We were all tired and hungry.

The nurse who helped me couldn't find her lunch money. She searched to no avail. After she cleaned Victoria up, took her vitals and prepared to clean me up, she rolled me onto my side, and guess what was sticking to my rear end? Her lunch money! We all laughed so hard. I told her because it was stuck to my rear end, it was my parting gift and she would have to eat the hospital food for lunch.

She laughed and said, "No way. I'm going to clean this money up and go out and get me some lunch. I've worked hard for this money, honey." With that, she wiped it off, sanitized the money, and went to get her lunch.

I wasn't prepared for how tired I would be after the delivery and the fact that this gorgeous baby doll was put in the room with me. I had to feed my new bundle of joy, change her diapers and be totally exhausted after delivery and through out the night. I wasn't prepared for the fact that I would have pain from an episiotomy for two weeks and a sagging pooch for a tummy up to three weeks after delivery.

I also wasn't quite prepared to have a nocturnally motivated party creature, I mean, angelic baby girl, who only slept for small spurts of time. I would often fantasize about sleep because it was something that eluded me. I often wondered how such a beautiful girl could survive on such little sleep and why she didn't allow me any. I thanked James continually for his great help and effort in letting me sleep for small spurts of time while he bonded with Princess Victoria.

So many things I wasn't prepared for, yet I had some of the best side effects of the process. I had little morning sickness, except nausea in weeks 9-11. I was very active and worked every day until I delivered. Unlike pre-pregnancy, I started having regular bowel movements (sorry if this is too much information, but it was an anomaly for me). I had a true pregnancy glow and felt so great during pregnancy. I realized that it was such an amazing experience.

My labor and delivery were under eight hours. I eventually regained my strength and found times to sleep both during the day and night. I knew James was happy that I never got a ton of crazy or off-the-wall cravings. My biggest Achilles heel was watermelon, orange juice, salad, and shrimp. I just couldn't get enough of any of them and probably ate my weight in each of them. I also discovered the feeling of what it was like to have a tiny human being growing inside me and the joy of being able to see her for the first time. There are more loving and touching moments, but these are the ones that made it all worthwhile.

JIMMY'S STORY

Jimmy's story is probably the funniest of all the children. His was a complete surprise pregnancy (not that Victoria was planned). We weren't NOT trying. A friend once shared the saying with us, "If you're not NOT trying, then you're trying!" Victoria was one-year-old when I found out we were pregnant again. However, this time, I knew exactly when I got pregnant, down to the week. I was exactly two weeks along when I knew for sure. It wasn't because Mother Nature cooperated: I became more aware of my body and the change that had taken place within me. I waited for about a week to tell James, and boy was he surprised.

At this point, James and I decided that he should get a traditional job. Through his work as our company's financial officer, he discovered that he really enjoyed the financial sector and wanted to be a financial advisor on a full time basis. It was none too soon because we needed health coverage at an affordable rate for the three, soon to be four of us. I continued with our real estate ventures and property management firm. It was hard work, but it paid the bills.

My pregnancy with Jimmy really was great, minus the first 11 weeks, where I had morning sickness all day and night. I think whoever coined the term "morning sickness" severely underestimated time of day and had quite the misnomer. It can be an all-day event that just doesn't let up. However, starting with week 12, it was a breeze. I had a great pregnancy and the biggest lesson was to make sure to walk. I walked nearly two miles every day and drank over 80 ounces of water. I was pregnant in the summer, so I mall-walked and walked during the evenings to stay cool.

What made Jimmy's story so incredible was the actual day of delivery. I had been having a relatively normal day at the office and before I left, planned out the next day's activities. I was organized, so

I had a list going of things I still needed to get done. Jimmy wasn't due for nine more days, so I felt confident knowing I still had time to complete lingering tasks.

Around 3:15 am, I awoke to a feeling of nausea. I originally chalked it up to false labor because I needed more time and wanted to get more things done. I tried to lie on the couch and let James remain asleep until I thought it was important that he woke up to help me time the contractions. That thought lasted all of 10 minutes when I realized that the contractions were one long continuous contraction that wouldn't let up.

About 3:30 am, I realized I was actively in labor and going to have the baby soon. I attempted to breathe slowly and deeply as I moaned and paced around the house. I was sweaty and hot and needed to take a shower to cool off. I was in and out within two minutes because of the intensity of the pain. I have a high pain tolerance, but this was different and I wasn't ready for it. Then I felt like I had to bear down. I stepped out the shower, leaned my back diagonally against the wall and for the first time, felt relief. I finally found a comfy position. I was leaning there for about three minutes when I was suddenly pulled from out of my mental and physical comfort. I heard James slightly freaking out about seeing blood on my legs. We read enough books and knew enough to know that something wasn't quite right.

He called 911 at 4 am and the operator told him to get me out of the bathroom and onto the bed because I was in labor. The operator dispatched emergency personnel to our home while she was on the phone with James. I tried to fight her directions because I was finally comfortable, however my son's safety was of the utmost importance. I pulled myself from the bathroom to the bedroom and onto the bed. I was in labor at home and the only ones there were 20-month-old Victoria, James and I. It was time to put our carefully crafted birthing plan into effect. James made a call to his best friend J.Imoh and asked him to come and get Victoria because we had to make a mad dash to the hospital. Imoh lived about ten minutes away, and we lived about seven minutes from the hospital. Unfortunately, it was so early in the morning and he was so exhausted, he fell back asleep until his wife Marie nudged him and asked him who had called.

Imoh groggily relayed this message to Marie. "Victoria's in labor. We have to pick up Dee." Ladies, never give information to a man who is half asleep; who knows what will come out of him!

Laundry Can Wait

Thankfully, Marie knew what he meant; she jumped out of bed and drove at breakneck speeds…I mean, speed limit to our house.

It was scary for a few minutes as we waited for emergency assistance to arrive. Neither James nor I knew quite what to do first. Should we boil water and get towels ready, or would we have enough time to get to the hospital? What were we supposed to do with the water anyway? We started getting towels ready just in case, and I practiced my breathing and loud groaning.

At 4:15am, a volunteer emergency fire fighter heard the dispatch on his radio that a woman was in labor and needed assistance. He lived in our community, about a mile from our house. He rushed to the house and, at 4:20am, he knocked on the door. James answered it and breathed a huge sigh of relief. His prayers had been answered as he had been walking around half panicked and praying as he attempted to remain calm.

At 4:25am, the towels and extra sheets were spread out across my bed, and I was getting ready to deliver my son at home. That was a little freaky because as wonderful a moment as it was, all I could think about was how much blood would soak through to the mattress. Would my bed be ruined and we'd have to buy a new one? How much would that cost? Why, in the movies, did they always say to boil water? Would James remember to throw the linens and my nightgown in the washer so the stains didn't set? Would having this volunteer fire fighter and neighbor seeing me "in all my glory" embarrass me? Would it be awkward having to wave hi later on? I was confused and in pain. That was not how we had planned our second child's birth.

Then came a second knock at our door. It was Marie coming to get Victoria. Then, the ambulance showed up and blocked her car in the driveway. As Marie and Victoria stood in Victoria's room listening to me scream; I mean groan; the volunteer fire fighter said, "Don't push." I told him it wasn't me pushing. The baby was ready to come out. "Ready? Uh oh, there's his head. Push!" With that one push, at 4:28am, James M. Cadet, II was born. Jimmy weighed 7 pounds 15½ ounces and was 20¾ inches long. The two male EMTs were now ready and entered the room at 4:30am. Jimmy was already here and having a blast.

In our small Texas town and hospital, I was the first mom who had an unplanned at-home birth, in over 10 years. I became the talk of the little town and hospital. I was so calm that the EMTs thought something was wrong with me.

Laundry Can Wait

As they wheeled me through the living room on the gurney, I looked over and saw the front door open. I yelled back to my husband, "James, don't forget to lock the front door." As they rolled me through the kitchen and laundry room, I again called, "Honey, don't forget to take the sheets off the bed and put them in the washer." I expressed my gratitude to Marie, "Thanks Marie."

The EMTs kept looking at me as though I had somehow fallen down and bumped my head, and one of the guys asked me, "Ma'am are you sure you're all right?"

I sarcastically smiled and answered in the calmest voice I could, "I just had a baby. I didn't just hit my head!" I laughed, and they did too. I guess they realized that women are capable of anything and are fully prepared for what life throws our way.

In the ambulance, I finally exhaled as I looked over at my precious young man who couldn't wait to get here. We believed he was so excited to meet us that he heard the word "ready" and took that as his cue to make his grand entrance.

Later that morning, I had nurses and doctors stopping in to look at the woman who had delivered her baby at home. It became awkward and I had to ask them to stop doing that. My doctor came in laughing and said, "So you decided to do it without me this time, huh? I heard about the delivery before they officially called me in."

At 9am, my office was supposed to open. Obviously that didn't happen and I asked James to get the laptop from home so I could finish my remaining work, reply to e-mails, and tie up loose ends.

One of the nurses walked in and said to James, "Oh my goodness, is she some sort of crazy workaholic? I mean, she just gave birth."

Without batting an eye or missing a beat, James told her, "No, ma'am, she's just a successful business woman who has things that still need to get done. Are you about to take the baby and conduct a test?" (I love my husband.)

Can you imagine the site I must have been? I was lying in the hospital bed, IV drip connected to my arm, baby in the bassinet and me working on the laptop, about to answer my cell phone. Talk about a modern woman. That modern woman image was one that would carry me for a long time. However, as my future pregnancies developed, I was neither quite as modern nor ready for what would happen next.

OLIVIA'S STORY

When I became pregnant with Olivia, I was a little stressed. Victoria was four and Jimmy was two years old. We had made our move from Texas to Arizona less than a year earlier. I was reeling from being a mother of two toddlers learning how to be a stay-at-home-mom. James' job had him traveling several nights a week and the children and I were home alone with no family around, and only a small number of friends. We finally began to get ahead of our bills and debt as we adjusted to our new surroundings. I had also interviewed for at least two jobs without a final offer of employment on the table.

I had barely begun to get a handle on things when I found out I was pregnant with our third child. Honestly, I was not ready for another baby. I know that amazing moms do it all the time, but the thought of three children under the age of four was a rather inconceivable notion for me. Sadly, I did not know if I had enough love for a third child. I know that moms have a never ending reservoir of love, but I wasn't sure if I did.

The dynamics of our family were comfortable and everyone had their roles. It was a little scary to think of it all changing, on top of just having moved and James' new hectic travel schedule. I got involved with a couple of mommy groups, and I thought I was finally in control of my schedule and life. I wasn't ready to be completely unnerved and unraveled from what I thought was "control" and "functionality."

I knew something was amiss when I started feeling queasy and nausea came over me at the sight and smell of certain beloved foods. My heart sank at the idea of being pregnant, even though I enjoyed the experiences and beautiful children resulted. I reluctantly took the test and got the result, "+," but it was very faint and hard to make a definitive declaration. However, we all know what "+" means. I took the test again and got another "+," but it was still faint. So, I waited until the next day and bought another test. Again, "+," but it was still faint by my standards.

I hope you're keeping track because that is three so far. I waited until the next day, and first thing in the morning, "+." With the fourth test, I knew it was confirmed. I couldn't figure out how I missed any signs of being pregnant until three days before taking the tests. I knew down to the day when I conceived Jimmy. I thought I "knew" my body. I told James, and he was as surprised as I was. We had to strategize because he was traveling often with work and we didn't have any relatives close enough for us to be able to rely upon.

In the midst of adjusting to this new discovery, one of my uncles passed away. I had not seen him or other family members in over 20 years. It was a sad occasion for me, but I flew to North Carolina to attend his funeral and visit with my father's side of the family. While there, I learned that my last remaining uncle on my father's side of the family was terminally ill and not expected to survive longer than six months. We spent a weekend reconnecting and forming new bonds and memories. After the funeral and weekend with my N.C. family, I flew back home to Arizona.

I made a doctor's appointment when I got back to Arizona, and my new physician confirmed my pregnancy. Things were still relatively early along, but because of the high stress I experienced over my uncle's death, she advised me to take things easy. I worked to do that, but with a two-year old and four-year old running around, that was a tall order. In addition, I enjoyed going to the gym and working out to ease my frustration. I knew I couldn't give all of that up at once.

Nearly a week after that appointment, James and I went on a date. Upon using the restroom, I noticed "spotting." It was light, but made me concerned. I decided to carry on with the evening anyway. However, when I got home, I took another pregnancy test to ease my mind and "+" was the result. I called the doctor on Monday morning, and she told me to minimize all activities unless absolutely necessary. A week later, I had a second doctor's appointment and again, the "spotting." At this point, James and I became increasingly alarmed. We didn't know what this meant or why this was happening. I took a final pregnancy test, and it was a faint, "+."

Within two weeks from the initial "spotting" incident, I experienced the worst side cramping I could remember. Instantly, all the pain and discomfort of childbirth flashed back to my mind and I was reminded of what it felt like to be in labor. I tried to settle my mind and think positive thoughts as I prayed. Thankfully, my body settled down and all the cramping stopped. I called the doctor, went into the emergency room and was put on strict bed rest. I was to stay in bed and avoid stairs until further notice (impossible because we lived in a two-story house and I cared for two active children). James decided to take a week off from work and help out. I called my three closest friends and asked if they could take the kids for play dates or sleepovers for that week.

Towards the middle of that week, I had the pains again. I prayed, e-mailed, and called those who were great at prayer. I took a warm bath. I walked. I cried. I doubled over. Nothing would help. I gave birth to my baby girl Olivia, at home. I cried for hours before calling my OB. Again she instructed me to go to the emergency room. She also asked me to put the stillborn remains of my baby in a plastic bag and bring the bag with me to the hospital so they could run tests to make sure everything was OK with me.

It took superhuman strength, and I had to mentally check out, but I did it. To this day, I still wonder how I was able to put my baby in a bag and ride with her in my hands all the way to the hospital. James drove the kids to a friend's house and dropped them off. Then he and I went to the emergency room. I sobbed uncontrollably and again, fell apart, in his arms while we waited to be called. Never have I felt or known the emptiness I felt that day. I dreamt about meeting her. I envisioned laughing with her, teaching her to walk and eat, her first day of kindergarten, and James and me walking her down the aisle on her wedding day. So many things I wanted for her that I would never get a chance to see or do.

I was devastated. I slumped into a depression for nearly three weeks. I just didn't know what to do. I couldn't eat, sleep, or get myself together. I blamed myself. Again, thoughts of overdoing it with kickboxing and aerobics plagued my mind. Did I stress over family and my husband's job too much? Did I not eat right? Why wasn't I aware of my body and the things that were going wrong?

So many questions, and the only answer that stuck in my head came from my OB. She tried to ease my mind and allay my blame and fears. She told me, "These things just happen sometimes and no one really knows why. It's not your fault. Don't blame yourself."

I needed answers and was not comforted. I still questioned why this had happened and if there were more I could have done. I asked myself the fated question, "Why did this happen to me?" Perhaps taking six different pregnancy tests was my way of doubting to the point of causing hormones to hurt my baby. I didn't have an answer then, or now. The true reality is that I don't know why, and it's futile for me to look for what is an unanswerable question.

After three weeks of being fully depressed, I called one of my friends. She explained that she, too, had a miscarriage the previous year and knew what I was going through. She picked up the kids and took them to her house for the weekend.

Kelli, another dear friend and spiritual leader I reached out to, confided in me that she also had a baby pass on, except her baby girl was carried to term. Her daughter had been diagnosed with health conditions in utero. She survived delivery, but shortly after being held by her parents, she passed on. My heart was broken for Kelli. My dream of holding little Olivia was so real, but I couldn't imagine holding her fully developed body, only to have to say goodbye so quickly. When I asked Kelli how she was able to deal with it, she told me, "GOD! He is the only one who can help and heal you." I took her words to heart and realized that whether a life is 12 weeks old in utero, five minutes old outside of the womb, or even 25 years old, they are still a life and a parent mourns. It comes down to the heart of hopes and dreams we each have for our children.

Once my heart healed, I promised myself that I would take the time to enjoy Victoria and Jimmy. I also promised God that if He were to allow me to have another child, I would take each day as a valuable treasure and enjoy every moment that I had with my children. I made a point to realize that every child is a precious and cherished gift, and I would not squander any future opportunities. My new perspective showed me life is but a vapor, and if I blink, I might miss it.

That was the promise I made. As a parent, we should all consider making this promise. We get so busy with life that we forget that children are a blessing. We overlook that each age is a different stage that will come and go before we know it. I challenge you to learn to cherish the life you have been entrusted with and take special care of your little ones.

Because of this experience, I gained a newfound appreciation for my children and how much they mean to me. I picked myself up, dusted myself off and began to walk in the joy of being a mother as I prepared for my new adventure and new mindset.

GABRIELLA'S STORY

A year after Olivia passed, I decided it was time for me to start a new phase of my life. I had stopped going to the gym and I decided it was time to get back in shape. When I worked out and ate healthy, I was happier and more relaxed. Exercise relieved stress and gave me an overall glow. I joined a diet-based website and learned what it took to lose weight. I became dedicated to a lifestyle of healthy eating and making exercising a part of my daily routine. It was wonderful because I joined a message board where others kept me accountable to my goals and challenged me to be my best. It worked. I lost 20 pounds in five months, and I looked and felt better than I had in years. I was near my pre-marriage weight, which was exciting to me, especially after having been pregnant three times.

In the last "message board challenge" before the Thanksgiving holiday, I noticed that the smell of chicken was making me sick (poultry and seafood are the only meats I eat). That night at dinner, my throat was sore and the sight and smell of salad almost made me want to hurl. I pressed through it thinking I had a flu bug.

Thanksgiving at our house with my in-laws was in full effect. I hated the thought of being sick and tried to take extra vitamin C pills to boost my immune system while I ate soup and drank tea. My efforts did not work, so I went to the doctor. I found out I had a severe case of strep throat. I was on antibiotics and quarantined to my room. My mother-in-law cooked, took care of the house, and helped James with the children while I was sick and she was on vacation.

We were sad to see my in-laws leave. Everyone enjoyed their visit, especially the children. While my in-laws were at our house we joked about their love of spoiling our children. We wondered who these people were and where they had been when they were raising us. It seemed that our parents were too busy raising us to be great people, to indulge the whims and fancies of children. However, now they have nothing but time, toys, and sweets in their role as Nana and Papa!

To add insult to injury, a week after my in-laws left, I was walking down the stairs in a medicine-based fog and carelessly missed a step. I tumbled down the staircase causing black and blue marks from my knees up to my back. I was absolutely miserable and had to stay in bed for another week.

It was not until a week before Christmas that I realized my sickness wasn't going away. My strep throat was healed and my body felt better, minus the bruises from falling down the stairs. However, the smell and sight of chicken and salad still made me sick to my stomach. Now, it seemed, I loved the taste of milk and wanted it by the gallons. Since this was extremely odd behavior for me, I took a pregnancy test. Never had I seen results appear so quickly. The very first test was a very strong and dark "+." There was no need for a second test. I showed James, and we were both overjoyed. We prayed and talked for what seemed like hours, in an effort to mentally prepare ourselves for our new journey.

My daily prayer went something like this: *"Lord, help this child to be joy-filled and healthy. Help me to enjoy this pregnancy and have a safe and speedy delivery. Help this baby to grow strong and healthy while in my womb, and protect him or her from childhood sickness and disease. Allow this baby to be a joy to our family and each of us to love and embrace him or her. Let this precious gift be filled with laughter and good cheer and reveal his or her destiny to me as he or she grows. In Jesus' name I pray, Amen."*

I prayed that type of prayer daily to remind myself of the promise that I made to both myself and to God. I reminded myself that the life growing inside of me was a beautiful and precious gift that I could not automatically assume would have no issues or problems. I prayed this prayer to ease my heart and mind and comfort me in knowing that THIS was a different pregnancy and I should expect different results.

I called my OB the next day and made an appointment because she had been comforting and readily accessible the previous year. I trusted her and knew that she would help me through anything. The first thing she did was an ultrasound. She made sure that all was well. Not only was everything good, I was already two and a half months pregnant and didn't have a clue. I had to laugh because God truly had a sense of humor this time. I had lost 20 pounds and could finally fit into my skinny jeans, and now I had to prepare to gain it all back. It was news I certainly welcomed and loved hearing.

Through the process, I cherished each bump, curve, kick, chocolate bar or cup of cocoa. I learned not to complain as much and realized that with each passing day, my baby was growing stronger and healthier. I looked forward to hearing her heart beating or seeing her on the ultrasound. Gone were the thoughts of concern over family dynamics and roles. My love for this new baby deepened, and I learned to take each day in stride and cherish every moment. Subsequently, my friend and pastor, Kelli, also found out she was pregnant with her fourth child. She and I were able to go through our pregnancies at the same time. She and I faced our separate challenges, fears and joys together.

On one occasion, when the lab told me that I tested positive for having Downs Syndrome, I called Kelli slightly unnerved, and we prayed. I immediately felt peace. The Spirit of the Lord said to me, "The test results are wrong. Retake the test." I was reminded of the time when I was pregnant with Jimmy. I had to take a three-hour glucose test because I had been diagnosed with possible pregnancy-induced diabetes. I told the lab technicians that I didn't have diabetes. When I was pregnant with Victoria, I passed the one-hour test without a problem. I was not sure why I didn't pass the one hour with Jimmy. When the results of the three-hour glucose tests came back negative, I smiled at the lab technicians, walked out and felt vindicated. This memory encouraged and strengthened me.

At the next OB appointment, I reviewed all the test results with my doctor. I boldly told her that somehow the positive test results for Downs Syndrome were wrong. She looked at the test results and chart for nearly ten minutes and couldn't figure out how the results could be wrong. It was towards the end of the appointment that she thoroughly examined the chart and realized that one of the new girls had made a mistake and miscalculated my due date. The reason for the false-positive result was that I had taken the test too early. She profusely apologized. I was scheduled for a new test sequence, and she personally checked all test results from that point forward. Once the new results came back, they were well within allowable range, and all was well. Having my doctor on my side listening to my concerns, ensured a great relationship and built trust.

The rest of the pregnancy with Gabriella was enjoyable. I decided that even though I couldn't get into my skinny jeans, I would buy fashionable clothes that celebrated being fit and pregnant. I told James I was going to be the hottest, sexiest pregnant momma he ever saw. And I was, thank you! I gained a total of about 23 pounds. I was literally "all baby," until the 9th month. I guess my joking that God had waited until I lost 20 pounds before He blessed me with another baby was a good thing.

I stayed in shape by drinking about 80-100oz. of water daily and walking or doing very light exercises. I even bought a two-piece bathing suit, (not something I would normally do). It was so hot in Arizona that I couldn't help it. The only way to stay cool was to sit in the air-conditioned house or swim in the pool. I'd go from house to pool. Either way, I was happy.

On July 2nd, I made a deal with Gabriella. Either she would have to come before July 2nd, because we scheduled a big pool party, or she would have to wait until after July 4th. She was due on July 7th. She responded by wriggling and turning over. I didn't know what that meant. On July 4th, we had our pool party, and as the fireworks were going off, I started feeling Braxton-Hicks contractions. Nothing major that couldn't be walked off, but they were there regardless. Looking back, I think Gabriella realized that there was something fun going on and she wanted to be a part of it. By the end of the night, she had settled back down and was comfortable.

July 5th and 6th came, and no real movement, just discomfort. My OB and I had discussed inducing me if my due date came and only partial movement occurred. I showed up to the hospital on the morning of July 7th. My initial exam showed me at three centimeters dilated. That was more than enough for me. If Jimmy's process served as any example to me, I could labor and deliver all within an hour. We didn't want to chance being sent back home, so my doctor willfully admitted me.

Despite basic explanations, I didn't have a clear picture of the "induction" process. Inducing me meant the nurse would break my water and give me Pitocin to make my contractions stronger. These stronger contractions would help push the baby down the birth canal. I had a birthing ball, which was amazing and allowed gravity to do its thing. I went from three centimeters to nine centimeters in about 45 minutes. That's when the nurse made me lay down and gave me something called Staydol to help me rest. I hated that medicine because, as James said, "I behaved like a sloppy drunk." Despite being partially coherent, I was fully aware of what was going on around me. The nurse said it was supposed to take the "edge" off the contraction and allow me to rest. I barely rested, and the edge must have been paper-thin because I felt the pain. That is, until I got that wonderful epidural. I was finally able to concentrate more on pushing and less on pain aversion.

Eight hours after being checked into the hospital, my OB joked, "I thought your labors were supposed to be short! I see you got your toenails done in purple today. Somehow women always manage to get their toenails done just before they deliver."

We had a good laugh because she and I both knew I could neither see nor reach my toes, nor did I have time to go to the nail salon. My very talented 6-year-old daughter Victoria had picked that color and painted my toenails. Even funnier is that my female OB noticed. My male OB never noticed a thing. I guess that is why women are women and men are men.

Gabriella was proving to be one tough little cookie that day. She was none too happy about being evicted from her comfy surroundings. She eventually decided to be delivered four hours after active labor began and came out looking at the doctor fully "sunny side up."

Even at birth, Gabriella was taking names and memorizing faces. She wanted to know exactly who to come after for making her come out of hiding. She definitely made her personality known and showed us she was so much more than what we had prayed for. Gabriella weighed 8 pounds 6 ounces and was 23 inches long.

I would say that there are several morals to be taken from each of these stories:

1. Although I had a plan for each birth, I ultimately had to consider what was best for the baby regardless of what my plan entailed. I had to be realistic and adjust to the situation and the baby. Health trumps plan any day.
2. I had to train my mind to think positive in spite of all the stories I had heard or situations that were presented. Having an optimistic attitude produced a favorable effect on everyone I encountered.
3. I learned to find someone who could be a role model by giving me wisdom and guidance.
4. I discovered I initially needed only 100 extra calories a day in addition to a healthy diet. Later, I ate small healthy snacks, and drank plenty of water and exercised, because it made labor much easier to bear.
5. I learned to trust my doctors and also my body. It was necessary to discuss all types of contingency plans so that I was aware of how and what the OB believed and how they proceeded in unforeseen or emergency circumstances.
6. The pain of childbirth does go away. However, when I got ready to deliver the next child, I was always reminded of the depth of pregnancy discomfort.

Although my birth stories are relatively uncomplicated, I want to emphasize that each child is different. This is not a license to completely wing it, but you have to be able to adjust to a change in plans. Our goal as parents should always be to keep the children as our priority and do what is best for them.

My challenge to all moms is to think about funny, eventful, or important moments of each of your children's pregnancies and deliveries, and chronicle your own thoughts. To the moms-in-training, think about what kind of pregnancy and delivery you would like to have. Write down your thoughts and recite them daily so that you begin to speak and create the environment you want to happen.

Whether you are new, seasoned, or in training, find a role model. Find a woman or group of women whom you can learn from and get advice, thoughts, or sometimes even a reality check. It's important to surround yourself with women who exemplify what you desire to be, or even share in what you're going through. If you're a confident mom, take the initiative and become a mentor.

> *"Children are not casual guests in our home. They have been loaned to us temporarily for the purpose of loving them and instilling a foundation of values on which their future lives will be built."*
> – Dr. James C. Dobson

NOTES:

CHAPTER 3

AM I DOING THIS RIGHT?

"If evolution really works, how come mothers only have two hands?"

– Milton Berle

Confession time! As I begin to write this chapter, I feel so hypocritical. I just finished yelling at my kids, "Go upstairs, stop wasting water, get in the shower, use soap AND water, wash your bodies, get your pajamas on, brush your teeth and get in the bed!" My husband is away on business, and I'm slightly stressed out by their continual need to play, above all else.

However, I took a deep breath and said to myself, "I am the best mom in the world!" I pulled a Jedi mind trick on myself and forced myself to believe something I didn't necessarily feel. Do I feel that way all the time? No! Do I handle every situation with ease and expertise? No! I am human. I am human enough to get annoyed, but mature enough to ask for forgiveness for yelling at the kids. Yes, I did ask for forgiveness because I yelled out of frustration and irritation. I want them to know that I am out of line and don't want them to model this particular behavior. They need to know that wrong is wrong and you must apologize for wrong actions.

This begs the question of "Am I doing this right?" If I were Master Yoda raising a young Luke Skywalker and Princess Leia, I would know about the Force inside of me and how to tap into it to give me all of life's eternal answers. Alas, I am not, and you'll have to ask me in about 25 years! What I do have is the Spirit of Jesus Christ, and He continues to lead and guide me as I seek answers to daily questions.

I think the "Am I doing his right" question is one that plagues each of us, even grandmothers. Sometimes, we get lofty or even single-minded and think that there has to be an exact way of doing things right. First ask yourself, what is the definition of "right" and how do you quantify that? That which is right for me may be totally wrong for you.

We have to calibrate our mind to think with different parameters. We have to parent with the end in mind and think whether our actions today are going to foster or hinder the result that we desire out of our children. Yes, at that moment yelling at my children may have prompted them to move faster. However, the example that is left in their minds and hearts looks something like this: "When I grow up and become a mommy or daddy, I will have to yell at my children to get them to do the things I want them to do." Is this the impression that I want? No, hence the apology. Sometimes what is most expedient is not always the right thing to do for the long term.

Whenever I have to discipline the kids, I am reminded of when James and I began dating. He had what I deemed a "mountain-molehill philosophy." He would make a big deal out of the smallest situations. It didn't matter the scenario or how obscure the details, he would always look at the worst outcome and then he would proceed. In his training as a military intelligence officer of the US Army, he was trained to think this way for battle situations. It used to drive me crazy until I learned the wisdom in his thinking.

The wisdom is that you think of the worst-case scenario. Then you are able to prepare different contingency plans to escape the undesirable outcome. In essence, you can war-game some situations and do what you think is best, based on the information that you have at the time, as well as the desired outcome. Now, don't be rigid in this because the information presented may change, as well as what you desire to see as an outcome. You have to adjust to satisfy the needs of that present time. Navigating the bumpy road of discipline is a tricky task and one that will take specific knowledge of how your particular child reacts to consequences.

For example, Victoria has a soft heart and feels deeply. She works hard to do things right the first time and hates to make mistakes. However, she also has a very strong-willed and determined streak within her that is difficult to shake. If she has made up her mind to head down a path, right or wrong, she's going down the path full steam ahead. One day, she was doing her homework at the kitchen table and suddenly didn't feel like doing it any longer. She piddled around and wrote down anything and did it as sloppily as she could imagine. My philosophy is that if you put forth your best effort the first time, there is rarely a need to re-do, but if you make a mistake, take it in stride and persevere until you get the right answer. She insisted she wasn't going to do it. I insisted she would. I yelled, she cried. I got up. She stared out the window. I yelled again, she cried.

She explosively yelled at and scared Jimmy and Ella when they came near her.

This exchange went on for over 30 minutes. Finally, I stopped and thought about what I was doing and what she was doing. I began to apply James' mountain-molehill philosophy. Worst-case scenario meant no homework done, me angry with Victoria and Victoria getting punished or spanked. Best-case scenario was an accomplished Victoria and a proud mom excited to know my daughter is determined to do her best. Now, how to go from worst to best case with the least amount of turmoil? I stepped into my Obi-Wan Kenobi benevolent role and released her for 20 minutes to go and do anything she wanted to do. I informed her that after 20 minutes, I wanted her full attention. That did the trick. She had a long day at school and needed to decompress and didn't know how to relay that information. I avoided a mishap by stepping back from the situation to get clarity and gain control of myself.

Other times, this scenario played out with a stern warning and her being sent to her room until she apologized for her behavior. I had to figure out her heart motives. I had to determine whether she was challenging me because she wanted to see who was the Queen of the castle or whether she legitimately needed some time to herself. After having spent time observing her and Jimmy early on while we home schooled, I knew what her best was and I also knew when she couldn't care less.

The recap is that I initially yelled at her because I thought she was just being lazy and didn't want to do work. However, when I stopped and thought about our reactions, I chose to allow her some time because it was counter-productive to continue on the same course of action. I needed time to think about how to respond better and draw the positive out of her instead of running up against the brick wall. The solution here was to get her to do her homework to the best of her ability. That was achieved, but it took both of us stepping away from the situation to see more clearly and accomplish the task.

Jimmy, on the other hand is the total opposite of Victoria. Although he is as sweet as sugarcane, he is also extremely pigheaded and loves to play more than he likes to work. We can discipline Jimmy and within a matter of 30 minutes or less, he's forgotten about the infraction and punishment and repeating the problem behavior. Jimmy has done gymnastics moves in the house almost kicking his sister in the head and knocking over a glass vase. He is one who is doggedly determined to challenge authority figures to see just how far he can go. We have disciplined Jimmy and, in the midst of it, he gives the look like, "Is that all you've got?" I can remember one time where I had to spank him for being rude and disrespectful. After some time in his room, he came out, apologized for being rude and disrespectful, and then asked if he could play with Victoria in her room.

I overheard them talking. Victoria asked, "Jimmy, are you OK?"

Jimmy responded, "Yeah, I'm fine. It didn't hurt. I just cried like that, but it didn't hurt. Mommy's spankings don't hurt as much as Daddy's spankings."

Victoria chimed in with, "Yeah, Dad's spankings do hurt. It's good he doesn't give us many."

They both ended the conversation with sneaky, yet loud laughs. At first, I was livid. I wanted to go back in there and spank Jimmy again, and enroll Victoria in the program too. Instead, I calmly walked into her room and said, "So, my spankings don't hurt as much as Dad's huh?"

To wit they both said, "No Mom, your spankings do hurt."

"Well, just so you know, I think I'll find out what Dad does and start doing that. Thanks for letting me know." Since then, I have yet to hear anything more about that! The point here is not focused on spanking or other forms of discipline. The goal is to get to the heart of the child and help them to acknowledge their wrongdoing, apologize for it, and then look for ways to avoid negative future behavior.

On a separate occasion Jimmy and Ella decided to be young artists and draw on the hallway wall. The consequence was that they had to clean the wall, and Ella was not allowed to use crayons for two full days while Jimmy could not play his video games for a week. Note to moms; always buy washable crayons and markers. It will save you time, energy and a whole lot of sanity. Although I've also been told WD-40 and the Mr. Clean Magic Eraser both work well.

Although these examples are minor in the grand scheme of children's poor choices and things they and others have done, I felt it important to walk the dog and show how children's personalities and the level of the infraction both play in designing the most effective consequence that hopefully deters them from repeating that action.

We do not use corporal punishment as our main form of discipline. We implement a verbal and written chart. They understand that certain infractions of behavior will qualify them for "x" consequence…all the way up to corporal punishment. We normally follow this pattern. First we warn them that their behavior is going to lead to a poor outcome for them. If the behavior continues, we identify the wrong behavior, asking the child why they made that choice and what that wrong choice represents. We then ask the child to state in their own words what wrong choice and behavior was made. They state the consequences, then we administer those consequences. Afterwards, we reconcile with hugs and reaffirming conversation of our love for them but not condoning the behavior. Finally, we discuss how to improve their behavior by making better choices.

The moral is to learn how and to what your child responds. Then you should learn how to be effective and creative in the use of consequences so you can promote a high moral compass by correcting wrong behavior. The intent should always be to correct the heart of the child. It will manifest itself in correction of the behavior or in teaching children that actions have varying degrees of consequences. Always help them understand what they did wrong and why it was wrong. As children mature, their moral compass should tell them right from wrong. You will have solidified in their minds that they are separate from their behavior and they have a choice in their response to situations.

Most importantly, make sure to always support and highlight right behavior and choices. This will help you avoid getting into a cycle of rewarding for negative behavior. We have a reward chart that allows our children to gain rewards for positive behavior. They can perform helpful and considerate acts to diminish their consequences or gain special treats at the end of the week.

WE ALL MAKE MISTAKES

Yet again, this begs the question of "Am I doing this right?" I truly wish that, at birth, babies came with some sort of instruction manual tattooed to their behinds. As they grew, the instructions would change based on their age and needs. Instead of those meconium stains, instructions would be a nice gesture. I don't think any mom alive would protest. Just think, it would take the guesswork out of many of our questions. Will my child grow up to be the President of the United States or a lead singer in a band? When will my child grow up and leave the house and stay gone? What if, when they started walking, a price tag appeared on their foot telling us how much we would have to spend on their college tuition and post-graduate education? This way, we would know how much to save for their futures.

Alas, this is merely my "I wish" list. The truth is that it's all an educated guess based on our collective experiences of how we grew up, what we were told by family and friends, and what we were able to learn through reading, seminars, or learning by osmosis (just checking if you're reading intently here).

When Victoria was a baby, I would hold her in my arms, and stare so sweetly into her eyes. She would stare back at me with this quizzical look on her face, almost as if to say, "Hey, do you know what you're doing here?" I confess that sometimes we were just winging it and hoping we would make it through the day. Remember, I said earlier that my priorities for Victoria were: to make sure not to drop her, make sure she was fed and changed, and not go anywhere without her or leave her by accident. She was my very first baby, you know. I also wanted to ensure I got a shower at least every two days.

I remember when Victoria was about six months old. James, Victoria and I were all at our office. James and I were going between the front and back rooms and Victoria was in her car seat in the back office. He wanted to pick up his #2 girl (of course I'm his #1 girl), so he picked up the car seat and THWOOP! Out came Victoria face-first onto the rug. He gasped so loud and Victoria let out such a blood curdling mad scream that I came running from the front room and almost ran into the hallway wall. He was nestling her close, and tears began streaming down his face. He had dropped MY, I mean our baby. I was furious. I grabbed her from him and hugged her while we all cried. I couldn't believe that he was so careless as to have dropped MY baby girl. Once I calmed her down, James and I sat together holding her and promising we would take special care to never let that ever happen again. We snuggled her and let her know how sorry we were and how much we loved her. She had no bruising and was over the whole scene within a matter of minutes, but we were mentally scarred by the experience. The "don't drop the baby" priority didn't happen.

After the back-office incident, we were extra careful to double and triple check her car seat before picking her up. About a week later, she and I had a rough night because she decided it was more interesting to watch the stars followed by the sunrise, than it was to get a good night's sleep. James had gone into the office, and I needed to grab that coveted shower. I clumsily buckled her into her car seat and carried her into the bathroom. I got the water running and took a shower. Victoria was happily watching me until she got bored and wanted out of her seat. I got out the shower after about 10 minutes. I dried off, and went to pick up the handle of her car seat. THWOOP! There went Victoria for a second time in one week. I thought I had buckled her in snugly. Somehow, in my grogginess, I had forgotten to fasten the hooks completely, and she wriggled out of the fasteners. My heart was broken. I had no one to blame but myself. I felt like I had let her down and I was the worst mommy EVER! Worse than my negligence, when I picked her up, tears welled and rolled from her eyes and streamed down mine, she gave me this look like, "Et tu Brute?" Shakespeare never came more alive for me than at that one moment.

Victoria, again, we are so sorry. I know that, as you read this, you will probably freak out about it, but sorry. The goal is to breathe and know that we included this to show that we all make mistakes. I hope you can forgive Mommy and Daddy! Please? OK, now that we are over that part, I have to move on and get back to the book.

We may not have been perfect, but we were doing the best that we could at that moment. By the way, that situation never happened again to Victoria or the other children. We learned from our individual mistakes. I somehow thought that, since I was a mom and had a mommy gene that was nurturing and caring, I somehow was immune to making mistakes. Well, I sure as heck wasn't and still am not. As much as I wanted to say, "Oh, we would never do that or allow this or that to happen to OUR baby…" I realized that I was treading on serious ground. Things happened that were sometimes beyond my control, and no matter how much I willed them to not happen, they happened anyway.

EDUCATE YOURSELF

As part of knowing if you are doing this whole mommy thing right, I have a few very helpful and necessary tips and scenarios to run through. Some are purely theoretical, whereas others should probe you to think hard about "knowing what you know" and learning to educate yourself to avoid mistakes or even to become a better parent.

The first tip I think is the most useful. Few people ever tell new or even seasoned moms, to register for a CPR/First Aid course. If you have already taken the course, make sure to renew your certification annually or get a video that you can watch repeatedly. I am sure we can all understand why it is important, but just in case you have any doubts I'll describe a few of the advantages.

It will probably cost you less than $50 and take less than eight hours. If you think you don't have eight hours in your schedule to take a class, ask yourself this important question: can you afford not to? This small investment of time could potentially save the life of your child, loved one, or stranger. It is something useful that each of us needs to know. Call your local Red Cross, fire department, public service department, athletic club, or contact your local childcare facility to find out if they are offering the course as part of the teacher recertification process. As parents, it gives us comfort to know that the caregiver with whom our child will be cared for has these certifications, so why shouldn't we have them?

The second tip is to sign up for parenting classes or courses. No, a class cannot tell you how to be you, but it can help you gain skills and give you new techniques or methods that you may not have known or considered. Many times we have the false perception that by simply hearing and being in a class, we are going to be taught some sort of erroneous mode of parenting that cannot fit into our particular parenting style. That could not be further from the truth. In reality, when you were in high school or college, did one single class shape you into who you were to the extent you did not deviate from exactly what it taught? I doubt it. The same thing happens with taking a parenting class. We fill our arsenal of tools and create the ability to have diverse methods for our use.

To further enhance and make the need for education crystal clear, I am going to paint a picture of three physicians. If your child got sick, and you knew this background information, which doctor would you choose?

Doctor A is a man who studied at a local college and decided to go into medicine. In Dr. A's third year of college, he struggled in school and it was hard for him to get into medical school; he had to apply three times before getting in. Dr. A's IQ was measured at 105 (out of 200, with the average person measuring 100). After 10 years of medical school and residency (normally an eight year program), he finally graduated with a degree in pediatrics. He put in applications all over town and finally received an offer of employment at one of the best and well-known practices in the city. Dr. A's family is extremely well connected and pulled a few strings at the pediatrics' office to get him this job. He has worked exclusively at the office for six months. You bring your child in for care, and he is assigned to your child.

Doctor B is a woman who studied at the same local college as Dr. A, then went to a prestigious medical school and graduated within the normal eight-year program. Dr. B's IQ is 150 and she graduated in the top 10% of her class. After graduation, she decided to go to business school because she wanted to go into hospital administration. During the two-year business school program, she took four continuing education classes to keep her medical license from lapsing. After graduating from business school, Dr. B decided to work in an established pediatric office that needed a new doctor because the founding pediatrician was retiring and wanted to sell the practice. You happen to bring your child in on her second day of practice.

Doctor C is a man who went to an Ivy League college and then applied to medical school. Dr. C was a good student in college and got into a renowned medical school. His IQ is 135 and his performance in medical school was slightly above average, plus he was well liked and respected as a hard worker. He graduated from the medical program in seven years. However, Dr. C chose to go to a third world country for two years to practice medicine and work on finding a cure for juvenile diseases. Upon completion of his two-year "missions" work, Dr. C returned to the United States and worked in the pediatric unit of a famous children's hospital. He was subsequently invited to join a brand-new practice in town. You bring your sick baby into Dr. C on the sixth month anniversary of the practice being open.

Which physician would you choose for your child and why? In your mind, what makes that physician qualified to care for your child?

Please note that the above scenarios do not represent anyone in particular, or even generally. It is a collaboration of fictional background information that will prompt us to think more seriously about how much we prize education and experience in others and in ourselves.

Normally, you are never given this type of background information on the physician to whom you are taking your child. Usually, we ask for a friend's referral, or we may set up an "interview" with the physician who will be treating our child. We often take it for granted that all things are equal and once you have a medical license and insurance that everyone is on a level playing field. As shown here, there are different levels of "qualified" and if we knew background information, what would we choose if it came to the health and welfare of our most precious treasures?

That's the choice we make when we decide whether we choose to expand our potential knowledge base. Just because you have a child or two doesn't mean you are doing all you can do to be the best and live life to the fullest. Experience counts for quite a lot. However, if you have the chance to learn more beyond your personal skill set, would you? The "school of hard knocks" is real and important, but why learn a lesson that someone else can help you avoid?

I remember when James and I took a child-rearing course a few years ago. We found that we were already using much of the information presented. Some of the information didn't apply to us and we couldn't use yet. However, we did keep it for later use, as our children grew older. Other new information was presented that we were able to make work immediately within our family unit.

The year after we took the class, my mother, Myra, and teenage sister, Sierra, came to live with us in Arizona. Yes, I did say teenage sister. My mother had another child after raising five of us through adulthood. We often joke that my mother was having one serious mid-life crisis. Most people buy a car or go on a vacation, but my mother chose to throw herself back into the joys of motherhood.

After Sierra experienced several different behavioral eruptions, we suggested that Mom take the class. She was from the "school of hard knocks" and wondered how a course could help her raise her sixth child. It would be an understatement to say that she was dubious at best. After taking the course, she admitted knowing much of the information, but it was packaged in a way that made it new and relevant for her particular situation. She learned that although she had experience, she was at a different stage in her life. She needed a refresher course on the dynamics of teenagers and novel ideas of how to reward or provide consequences for different behavior. What she was able to learn by stepping out into an area that was "new" for her proved to help update her child-rearing skills. It also helped Sierra understand that Mom loved her and was committed to making sure she was being raised with a purpose.

As with the example of the physicians, where do you place yourself with regard to education and experience? Are you like Dr. A, who wings it or relies on others to do your job? Are you like Dr. B, who does a good job as a parent but only lives day to day and operates on your bank of knowledge? Are you like Dr. C, who goes above and beyond good parenting to learn diverse skills needed to become a great parent?

WILL I PERMANENTLY DAMAGE MY CHILD?

If you don't take classes, you yell or scream out of frustration, or have a minor safety mishap, are you destined to ruin your child for life? YES! Just kidding! No, you will probably not ruin your child. Yes, you will still be the best mom in the world, but you may have a harder time at parenting than others who decided to take a different route. Even if you don't want to take a class, pick up a book and educate yourself on various perspectives. Check out the internet and join several blog sites. Basically, don't be a lone wolf. Raising children has been done as a communal endeavor for centuries in many different cultures.

If you can remember the days of begging to go outside and having to be back in the house by the time the street lights came on, then you should know what I'm talking about. If you remember, either personally or through a friend's experience, of getting in trouble down the street at a neighbor's house, then having said neighbor call your mom or dad, and you got in trouble a second time; you understand the concept of the collective whole. If you can't identify with anything I just wrote, well, you missed out on some good times. It was a time when people knew and depended upon their neighbors. Not out of necessity, but out of trust and respect. We were responsible to and for each other. As kids, a promise was a promise. We "pinky swore" on it and "triple dog dared." I miss that time and wish there were enough of us out here who could restore that time within our community of relationships.

Your child will probably not remember every mistake you made during their childhood. However, they will forever memorialize whether they felt loved and secure and how you treated them. It is within a child's make-up to always want to see the loving and good side of their parents. Their resilient little minds and hearts have the ability to block out quite a lot, but it is our job to make sure that we instill them with more good than bad. Our goal as parents is to change and morph into Obi-Wan Kenobi or Jedi Master Yoda and be the all-knowing one who not only has mastered the art of the Jedi mind trick, but also who knows the secrets to the universe. Star Wars can teach us quite a lot if we are looking to learn. If the science-fiction thriller is not what moves you, then how about looking for the Holy Spirit as your teacher and guide? He has helped me and many others concentrate on becoming great parents.

With all that is within me, I believe we all possess the ability to be great parents. When we dedicate ourselves to learning and honing our craft, we elevate our children and ultimately ourselves.

> *"Nothing you do for children is ever wasted. They seem not to notice us, hovering, averting our eyes, and they seldom offer thanks, but what we do for them is never wasted."*
>
> – Garrison Keillor

Laundry Can Wait

NOTES:

CHAPTER 4

AM I IN CONTROL?

"You can't always control the wind, but you can adjust the sail."
   – Ricky Skaggs "Can't Control the Wind" Lyrics7

As you read, you may notice that I am someone who enjoys order and thrives on a schedule. Although I am not a "fly by the seat of your pants" type of girl, I have learned how to schedule my time so that I make time for fun stuff and spontaneity. I know, it's kind of oxymoronic to think of the two. I think that if I schedule my day, I will be able to control it. As much as I work on being consistent and taking control, phone calls from others add urgent and necessary things to my already overburdened to-do list, often interrupting my day. Couple that with a barrage of e-mails that need to be answered. What about the last-minute phone call from school saying my child is sick and needs to be picked up? If that doesn't throw me off, I still have a list of things that didn't get done yesterday or earlier in the week. Now top it all off with a stubborn toddler demanding I play with her during what should be her customary nap or quiet time. Do I really have control at all? Sad to say, but NO!

Let me clarify. I have as much control as is feasibly possible for a stay-at-home-mom. There are times that my perception of control seems to be neatly locked inside of a triple-reinforced super tanker with double-deadbolt, three-pound steel locks. However, all I have is a bobby pin and a dream of one day cracking it wide open. As much as I want control, it consistently eludes and taunts me. Does that sound familiar to anyone else out there?

I remember a time when I lived by my Franklin Daily Planner; I had it all in stride and checked off each item on my list. Thankfully, I still have days of planning where I get it all done. I even have "SuperMom" days where I get a head start on the next day's activities. I have not started planning less, just prioritizing more when planning. I am better able to adjust to daily disruptions. By nature, I am a planner and need the certainty of knowing what comes next.

Some days are better than others, and some situations are better than others.

One week in March, I was able to coordinate with my mother to babysit Ella while I went to get my hair done in preparation for my birthday dinner with James. I had planned to be at the salon for an hour or two. However, the stylist was 30 minutes late and there were three women ahead of me. I could have left, but I didn't want to be rude and make the woman who referred the stylist look bad. In addition, my hair would not have gotten done for my birthday, and that was not an option! I walked out of that salon for the first and last time after spending a very long and tedious four hours. All I can say is, lesson learned. I was definitely not in control of my schedule because, if I had been, the whole thing would have taken 30 minutes or less.

CONTROLLING CHILDREN

There is a difference between control and the realistic expectation that children behave. As young people, my children are expected to follow my direction and exhibit self-control. I am in the process of training them to rely on what is right and to have a strong moral compass. Until they consistently display right choices, I have to lead, guide, and direct them in the way they should go.

"Control" assumes the idea that you alone are the only factor in your child's life affecting them. As parents, we should be the primary influencers who monitor all others, whether positive or negative. There are hundreds of factors that contribute to our children's behavior.

Your children have their own personalities and desires and others influence them. Have you ever noticed traits or behavior in your children from you or your spouse, plus new ones you've never seen before?

If your goal is to control or create your "perfect child," you will be sorely disappointed. It is in our DNA to fight when we feel like we are being oppressed or controlled.

Remember, your children are only human. We all make mistakes and do things that are contrary to what we were taught. Considering these points should help you understand that there are many different factors in approaching behavior and behavior modification.

Have the expectation that your children will grow up to be amazing people. However, there is danger in creating unattainable standards that are impossible for your children to meet. Don't forget to include your children and their personalities in the equation. You have to include their strengths and weaknesses. For example, if I expected Gabriella to be able to get all the food from her fork to her mouth without dropping any, I'd be crazy. I have to take into account that she is still mastering hand-eye coordination.

Because my teenage sister, Sierra, lives with our family, we are able to help monitor her grades in school. Although we could have hoped she would make the dean's list by sheer will power alone, it would have been unrealistic knowing that her efforts had only produced B's, C's, and D's. It was not until she dedicated herself to focused studying and individual tutoring that her grades began to reflect her hard work. She eventually achieved ranking on the dean's list for several consecutive quarters.

What about Victoria and gymnastics? She has natural ability. Is it realistic of me to assume that after two years of taking lessons, she is ready to compete on the national level with gymnasts who have trained since they were three years old? No! She may be able to compete one day, but her current skill and maturity level do not support that idea.

Realistic aspirations should not be confused with control over your child. Our expectations should cause us to stretch beyond our comfort zone. However, it is important to be mindful of and consider our limitations. In setting attainable goals, there needs to be room for future growth.

RAISING CHILDREN

One day last year I was talking with a woman about raising children, and she said, "You haven't raised children until you've raised a teenager." I agreed until that thought marinated in my brain for a few weeks. My main parenting experience is of raising stubborn and very strong-willed toddlers and school-aged children. I do however have the unique experience of assisting my mother with raising my teenage sister, albeit, without the complete responsibility of her being my child. In a sense, we are a blended family and as any mother raising a non-biological child knows, there are unique challenges associated with this type of relationship.

To not negate going through the "terrific twos" or dwarf dealing with a very independent, headstrong child, or even one with special needs, I will reason that everyone's experiences frame their view. Not every child has a tough two-year-old stage, nor does every teenager have a rough and rebellious stage.

As a positive, I remember many times when one of the children helped a stranger pick up something they dropped. At school, if a classmate needed help or a sympathetic word, Jimmy or Victoria were the first to step in and offer their assistance. There were times when they gave me the biggest bear hug imaginable, followed by a huge smile and "I love you Mom." Out of the blue, they would do something I hadn't asked them to do. The best is when they share displays of love and admiration for one another, "You're so good at that. I love you. You're the best in the world!"

My children never went through any terrible stage. They did, however assert themselves on some points. I remember when Jimmy was two and Victoria was four years old. Victoria refused to take naps and would lie in her bed for her entire nap time and quietly play with her dolls. Jimmy would get out of his bed and noisily play with his toys. It got to the point where we had to remove his toys from his room. He would then lie on his rug playing with the lint. My children are not angels, but they have many wonderful qualities that override their negative choices.

I have friends whose children have been so stubborn as to refuse to eat, or gag until they got what they wanted. There are others who have refused to stop hitting, kicking, punching, or biting. There were even those children who would hurt themselves, run away, or attempt to burn the house down, and their parents didn't know what to do with them. The hardest part about dealing with young children is that they are not completely logical beings capable of higher thought. They only know what they want and they want it now! Similar are teenagers at times, but at least teenagers understand and can have and present a cohesive argument. Then again, I remember losing a few arguments to a very persuasive preschooler.

One Thanksgiving Day when Jimmy was four-years-old, he was given some cranberry sauce on his turkey. He said he didn't like cranberry sauce. We asked how he knew, as he had never had the sauce before. He clearly said, "I don't like cranberries." As we thought about it, we realized it was true. He doesn't like cranberries (dried or fresh) and has always refused them on his salad. He doesn't like them on his turkey. He doesn't like them on his salad. He doesn't like them here. He doesn't like them there. He doesn't like cranberries anywhere. Sorry, I got into a Dr. Seuss *"Green Eggs and Ham"* moment.

The other end of the spectrum, consists of wonderful teenagers. My sister is an example of what James calls a "typical teenager." She can be sweet, thoughtful, and caring, yet she can have serious attitude eruptions and make poor choices. She uses her street smarts in unconventional ways and, as James likes to say, her motto is, "It's never my fault." She has to constantly be reminded of what needs to be done. She has yet to understand how to set and distinguish between priorities and what's not important. She would rather stay up late watching television than get a good night's sleep and be rested for her test the next day. If you give her an inch, she wants to take a couple of miles. She hears selectively and then turns it into something that benefits her. However, it could be worse and tougher. James and I have mentored teens who were violent, on drugs, wound up in jail, failed out of school, were belligerent and disrespectful to adults, and even those who were suicidal.

I came to realize a few years ago that many of the problems that occur in children happen regardless of whether the child is a toddler or teenager. Every age is a different stage, and when we put the correct perspectives in place, we will see that there are challenges as well as rewards along the way. Although some challenges are harder than others, they are still a challenge. Just keep in mind that every child is not the same or destined to follow the same path. Children grow and evolve, so don't get discouraged or lose hope.

I believe that it all comes down to the relationship you have built with your children and your ability to read and understand them over the years. Considering my experiences as a mentor and youth minister, I believe the foundation of what was laid within them at an early age creates the springboard for the teen years. The teenage years are meant to be a culmination of how many times your child allowed you to take a sneak peek into their inner thoughts and emotions. If you were able to deposit wisdom during that time; if you connected with them at their level and understood what they were going through; and if they felt you listened to them and had their best interest at heart, then the relationship should be strong.

A person, whether two years old, 18 years old, or 30 years old needs to feel and believe they are in an environment that promotes love, security, and value. I am not proposing that you need to be your child's best buddy. You should provide strong parental leadership while guiding and helping them to navigate the uncertain waters of adolescence. Our jobs as parents don't stop when our children reach 18 or 21 years old. They are legally considered adults, but they will always be our children. It is our job and our responsibility to provide support, leadership, guidance, wisdom, and then friendship.

Yes, we all know that many of the same things our children struggle with were around during our youth. However, today things in school and outside the home are more overt and the pressures are higher. Even though you understand and know what your child is going through, keep an open mind. They have a new perspective and need your wisdom.

If you don't have the answer, don't shoot one off the cuff or act like you know it all. Validate their time and concerns and let them know what you think. If they don't seem enlightened, let them know you will seek alternative answers. Maybe you need to do some research and talk to a guidance counselor, other teenagers, spiritual leaders or your neighborhood police officer. Build a strong foundation in the early going, so that as your children grow older, you become friends and WANT to spend time with each other.

WHY CAN'T I JUST CHILL OUT?

I love the idea of just letting go and letting loose, but my personality keeps getting in the way. I want to relax like an old pair of jeans. I am learning that it's OK if every speck of dirt isn't cleaned up before I go to bed. I don't argue if the kids pile their clothes on the floor in their rooms, (as long as they clean it up on chore day). If Ella plays orchestra with all the pots and plastic bowls in the cabinet, it's delightful music. I minimize yelling at the kids as they run from room to room laughing and squealing in delight, taunting each other. I recognize that in order for Jimmy to get dressed in the morning, he has to wake up 15 minutes before the other children. Jimmy enjoys playing and going at a leisurely pace, and it throws his day off to be rushed. I have discovered I love using the Crock-Pot because we have a more pleasant day when I don't have to throw dinner together at the last minute. I allow the kids to solve their own problems (short of blood or wounds) and that constant yells of "mommy, Mommy, MOMMY" can be ignored. I major in the majors and NOT in the minors.

A great "mommy moment" happened recently when the kids were getting dressed for school. Victoria came into my bedroom telling me that Jimmy had just eaten a part of the wall (some peeling paint). I told her, "He couldn't have eaten peeling paint off the wall because there was nothing for him to eat, so please get dressed." Victoria quickly walked back to the bathroom.

Just then, I heard Jimmy's problem solving technique emerge. "Victoria, don't bother Mom because nothing is flooding, no one is hurt or bleeding. We can handle this by ourselves." Within me, I tried to contain the urge to run down the hall and hug him for finally listening to my words. Instead, I smiled, and retold the story to James. We laughed and gave each other high fives.

With all of that, it stands to reason that I am laid back. Guess again! I am working on it, but have not arrived yet. I watch different women and am instructed on things I can do better. I am not a super-crafty mom who can wing it and take everyone's imagination on a fun journey. I have to work hard at simply letting go. I constantly utter, "I can do this. It's a phase. Don't yell at them because you're going to miss it when they're too old to do that." I make mental notes and write it down on index cards placed next to my bed.

I need to have days where I learn what it means to go with the flow and not be regimented. I sit in the playground sandbox and avoid wondering if a cat has recently been in it or if germs are squirming around in it. I have resolved that I will give the children a bath when we get home, and allow them to play in the sand. I constantly remind myself that this is a phase, and once it's gone, it's gone forever unless captured on film. I tell my children, "I can't wait until you get ready to get married. I'm going to show pictures of you in the tub, and I have videotape of your exhibitionist phase." We all get a good laugh out of their shrieks and gasps.

Even though I like control, why does my world revolve around this concept? Plainly stated, without the idea of control, I would be lost. I need it to set parameters and use it as a guide to measure myself. How can I let it go? I still struggle with this area and have more questions than answers. I am at a place where the more questions I ask, the more confused I get. I've just stopped asking certain types of questions and started accepting the fact that some things just are. I am embracing the fact that I don't know it all and that I have yet to find all the answers. Maybe you have found your own answers, and I applaud you. Regardless, we need to keep pushing forward until we are in a place where we are comfortable yet striving to become better.

SHOULD I BE MORE FLEXIBLE OR STRICT?

Being flexible or strict can apply to so many different areas as parents. It all depends on your personality and the particular item. In our house, we have a few strict rules that don't get bent and some that are more flexible. There are certain words that we don't use because they make others feel bad, are rude and disrespectful, and are just not necessary (stupid, dumb, ugly, shut-up, idiot, etc.) These words are banned whether you live here or not.

There was an incident when we moved to a new area and my children befriended a neighborhood boy. In the midst of playing with the kids, the boy said the game they were playing was "stupid."

Jimmy and Victoria looked at him, looked around, and said to him, "We don't use that word in our house. It's mean."

The boy didn't quite get what he had done wrong and shrugged his shoulders and said, "Whatever. Can we play a different game?" I felt so good at overhearing this exchange because my kids not only got it, but they enforced it for their good as well as for others.

We also have an "eat all of your food" rule. However, this is a flexible rule because it depends on whether they ate a snack before dinner and how much of it they ate. It is also contingent upon how much we gave them to eat for dinner. We are teaching them that they should respect their bodies and only eat to the point of suppressing hunger and feeling content. It's hard sometimes because they want to be gluttons and have seconds of something because they fear there won't be any left for later, or because they ate too quickly and still felt hungry. Whatever the reason, our goal is to teach them about self-control and not being wasteful.

No child in our household will be able to participate in a boyfriend or girlfriend relationship until we have deemed that child mature (hopefully when they are in college). However, they are allowed to have friends who they spend time with, preferably in groups. We have some good-looking kids, so we are definitely going to have to monitor this on a regular basis (proud mama speaking, but it's true). When they have a crush on someone, we tell them to share their feelings by making a card, drawing a picture or making them cookies. My teenage sister is required to bring the would-be-male-friend to our house and then we must meet his parents. If all goes well, she and her "friend" are restricted to group outings only.

You have to recognize whether you lean more towards strict or loose. If you gravitate towards being strict and it works for you, great. However, if it is not producing the results you desire to see, maybe you need to loosen the reins a little. Those areas will have to be based on your tolerance level as well as the maturity displayed by your children in that or other areas.

In the workplace, if someone can do a job 75% as well as you can, then give it to them, and supervise them on how to get to 100%. Supervise, not micromanage, is the key here. At home, if your child demonstrates an aptitude for respect and responsibility for themselves and others, they may be ready for their first "friend." If your child is younger and shows they can handle an area, such as choosing their clothing or completing their work without you hovering, then step back and make yourself available for questions without imposing on their space, time, or talents.

If you are someone who is relaxed or loose and you prefer to have a hands-off approach, that's great too. However, the same goes for you. If you notice that your child is not meeting the minimum requirements, you may need to become stricter in certain areas. For instance, if your child is missing schoolwork assignments and their grades are suffering, you need to intervene. For the sake of helping and allowing your children to live up to their potential in school, you may need to ask them for their homework daily so you can check and sign off on their assignment as complete. You may have to even impose some consequence if their effort and grades don't improve.

Maybe your belief is that your children should just learn from their own mistakes so that they can have their own experiences from which to draw. That can work; however, you have to be keenly aware of your child's decision-making capabilities. If your children have not demonstrated the ability to consistently make good decisions, you may need to step in and assist them until they show proficiency. This may be another time where you switch from the *role* of monitoring, to becoming involved in the *job* of redirection as a parent.

I remember a time when my teenage sister kept choosing the wrong friends. One time, she received an in-school suspension for fighting because her friends said she was the main perpetrator. The problem was that she chose her friends despite warnings that they were not going to be good for her. She thought she was a better judge of character than we were, so she continued to hang out with them. When a second mishap occurred with these friends, we told her that she needed to choose new friends. To let her know the extent of our commitment, we told her that we would visit her school daily until we were assured she had chosen new friends. We also contacted her teachers, principal, and guidance counselor for their help. We met with some resistance, but in the end, she saw the wisdom of our words and made new friends.

When Victoria was in kindergarten, she started gymnastics and piano lessons. Initially, she had a rough transitional phase, and we were met daily with opposition in her completing her schoolwork. It had gotten to a point where I was so frustrated that I vowed to stop her doing all activities until she could produce a better effort towards her schoolwork. My children know that if I make a threat, it is not idle, nor am I going to back down until I see the results that I expect.

"Mommy, I'm sorry for not wanting to do my work. I will do my best from now on." With that one statement, her focus changed and she showed a marked improvement. Since then, we have had no problems with her understanding that a good effort on schoolwork is a prerequisite for participation in extracurricular activities.

When you can assess a situation and quickly decide whether leniency or fortitude is necessary, you can say that you have arrived at being the perfect balance of what your child needs. However, the one caution I make is that in the midst of balance, make sure you are consistent with principles. If something is always OK, then it should always be permissible. If something is not authorized, it should never be allowed, barring injury or potential threat to life, limbs, or others.

> *"You are searching for the magic key that will unlock the door to the source of power; and yet you have the key in your own hands, and you may use it the moment you learn to control your thoughts."*
> – Napoleon Hill

NOTES:

CHAPTER 5

PLAYGROUPS = ADULT CONVERSATION

> *"Women have a passion for mathematics. They divide their age in half, double the price of their clothes, and always add at least five years to the age of their best friend."*
>
> – Marcel Achard

HOW MUCH BABY TALK CAN ONE WOMAN TAKE?

When the kids were younger and we lived in Texas, the houses were separated by acreage. We didn't know our neighbors because they lived too far away. The only time we saw one another was when we honked our horns and waved as we drove down the road to our respective homes. I recall many a time when I would not talk to an adult all day until my husband called me on the phone or came home.

Being in the woods made me miss conversing with other adults. I entertained the calls from telemarketers so I could have an adult conversation. One time, a telemarketer told me she had to get off the phone! I went so far as to watch for the mail person just so I could rush out and see another adult and spend two minutes conversing with him. It was sad to think of how much I craved conversation and just how little of it went past:

"Mommy wants Toria to eat all her food."

"Mommy needs Jimmy to clean up his toys."

I never did the whole goo-goo gaa-gaa talk. I found it demeaning to myself and to the children. I even felt compelled to stop everyone I knew from doing it. I often told them to speak to our children the way they usually spoke so that the children learned grammatically correct language. One day while visiting my father-in-law, Jean-Claude, in New York, he asked 18-month-old Victoria how she did on the airplane. "Papa, I did fantastic!" He was shocked and impressed that she knew how to use this three-syllable word in the correct context.

Truthfully, I think this stemmed from my need to talk to someone throughout the day. If I wasn't going to talk with an adult, why not teach the children to respond? I think that idea backfired on me. Once the children were able to string more than two words together, they talked from sunrise to sunset and sometimes even in their sleep. It was so incessant with Victoria that I was excited when Jimmy was finally able to talk because they would talk to each other. Today, they are each other's best friends and talk about everything.

Once Ella came along and her speech progressed, she began to have full conversations, play with, and even taunt them. It's quite humorous to watch. In one breath she yells, "Jimmy, stop it. Leave me alone." About 30 seconds later, she sweetly says, "Sorry Jimmy. Love you. Kiss." It is so sweet.

The more I found myself wanting to converse with adults, the more elusive the opportunity. Though the children enjoyed playing with one another, that got old after a while. In Texas, we had gotten along well by setting up play dates between one or two other similarly aged children, as there were no organized groups that I was aware of in our town. Once we moved to Arizona and Tennessee we found established groups dedicated to moms and children. Playgroups totally revolutionized and transformed my mommy experience.

What made these groups so dynamic was the revelation they brought me that I was not an island unto myself. I met other women who experienced similar things to what I was going through and gave me suggestions on how to conquer my children's daily behavior challenges. It was great because the kids were able to play for free and get their energy out. I was able to sit back and exhale for a bit before I had to jump back up. I wish the playgroup philosophy had dawned on me earlier.

WHY DO I NEED A PLAYGROUP?

As a stay-at-home-mom, playgroups are a lifeline of communication and friendship. Sometimes we wonder if our children are being socialized enough or how our children would interact with others. If your children are not in school yet, this is the perfect environment to foster friendships among children or teach your children great principles. They learn a host of skills from sharing to consideration. I knew of one mom who had a developmentally challenged son who would often bring him into one of the playgroups so he could experience and learn what other children his age were learning.

Sometimes, it is important to immerse a child in a group with others their age or slightly older because they may begin to model and perform certain behaviors that may have taken them longer to develop by themselves. That can be positive or negative. For example, my children are all good eaters, and they encourage other children to eat food that they otherwise might not have eaten. On the downside, if my children are following the example of a picky eater, then they themselves become more prone to being picky and don't want to eat as heartily as normal.

If you are a working mom, you more than likely have put your child with a caregiver. Daycares and preschools are organized playgroups that focus on teaching educational and foundational principles, motor skills, and social cues in a guided and safe environment. You have to do your research to find the best environment that supports your child's learning style, culture, and offers the principles of your belief system.

A friend of mine has two school-aged sons. When she went back to work, she put her sons in a topnotch private school. One son thrived both academically and behaviorally, while the other struggled behaviorally and kept getting daily notifications, despite having straight A's. When they moved from one city to another, she enrolled her sons in a different, lesser-known program. Both her sons began to thrive academically and behaviorally. The first school environment was more regimented and primarily focused on behavioral cues, before academics. The second school environment focused more on developmental milestones and self-paced facilitated learning. The son that initially had behavior issues in the first school struggled because the school's educational philosophy clashed with his learning system. At the second school, he was allowed to explore different methods of learning and excelled because he was guided into a model that worked for his abilities as well as his personality.

Often, working moms don't have the luxury of taking extensive time off from work to determine the perfect school or daycare environment. She relies heavily on friends, neighbors, and coworker recommendations. If you notice that your child is having clashes at school, you may want to consider having a conference with the child's teacher, program director, and school counselor without the child being present. The key is not to enter into the meeting being a "mama bear." In other words, don't assume that your child is perfect and it's the teacher's fault. Enter with an open mind and come with suggestions of how the teacher or daycare provider can help your child improve.

This meeting will help you get a sense and understanding of the teacher and her observations of your child. With this type of open communication, all parties involved can successfully join in the goal of making your child's learning experience fun and productive. You may leave the meeting with a sense that your child does not work well with that particular teacher. Possibly, the school's philosophy is in contradiction to your ideals, beliefs or what is taught at home. Perhaps there are home situations affecting your child during school hours that the teaching staff need to be made aware. Ideally, you leave with the sense that you have created a team concept towards the education of your child. Whatever happens, know that you are your child's role model and advocate. School should enhance what is taught at home.

HOW DO I FIND ONE OF THESE FANTASTIC GROUPS?

Finding a playgroup can be as easy as turning on your computer and searching local mommy blogs. If you don't have a computer, pick up a parent magazine or local paper. You should be able to find a list of support groups based on your particular needs and desires. There are groups for stay-at-home-moms or working moms with infants, toddlers or a combination. There are groups for different ethnicities and for the city in which you live. There are groups for special needs or other abilities. There are groups for the affluent and not-so affluent. Whatever you need, there is a group for it. If, for some reason you cannot find a group, create one. Maybe there are moms out there who are just like you. If you have a "can only meet on Thursday" group, then do it. Pick a neutral, kid-friendly place that is free (park or mall), and go for it. You may have to create a flyer and pass it around as you're out and about. Perhaps you see the same group of parents regularly; strike up a conversation and make plans to meet at the same time and location the following week. The point is that you have to open your mouth and engage other moms.

Sometimes, a mom will see you in a random place and literally accost you (just kidding Natacha). I was taking a Mommy and Me swimming lesson with Jimmy when he was two years old. We were in the pool in the middle of swim class when a very pleasant, yet forward woman by the name of Natacha approached us poolside. "Excuse me, Miss, but my friend and I are a part of a new local mom's group, and I wanted to give you our card just in case you may be interested in meeting with fellow moms for a playgroup." At first, I was cordial and almost dismissed her. I mean, where in the heck was I supposed to put a business card in the middle of the pool? Truthfully, I was very happy she approached us. I was new to the area, in need of a break, and looking for a way to meet other moms.

She and a few other women had just formed the Mocha Moms of the East Valley. Natacha opened the door to a dynamic group of women who had similar interests to ours, and I was excited when we attended the playgroup. We joined the Mocha Moms and have maintained friendships with many of the families regardless of life's situations. I am truly thankful that she approaching us that day.

Sometimes, it takes being bold, yet friendly to meet the needs of a mom. Have you ever been anywhere with the children, or even by yourself, and seen a mom who looked like she was struggling and in need of a long overdue break? (I just raised my hand, sorry!) She needs someone to throw her a life preserver. Next time, encourage her with a smile. Offer to buy her a cup of coffee or smoothie. Moms need to know that there's someone out there who appreciates them, knows what they are going through at that moment, or let them exhale for a few minutes.

Some mom groups will cost you a nominal fee ($20 – $60/year) to join while others are free. If there is a fee, it is worth it, considering all that you are getting out of the group. Paid annual membership fees are used to offset things like: buying arts and crafts or holiday party supplies, supplying new mom gifts, and sending get-well baskets. Have I sold you on the idea of joining a mommy group? Just in case you need further affirmation, here are a few other things to consider.

Mommy groups need the talents and skills of all kinds of women. Maybe you're a great artist or craft person and can teach other moms how to do these things with their children and make their mommy-child time together more fun. Are you great at organizing and can help schedule playgroups and get everyone together? You may be a social butterfly and can help expose other moms to the joys of playgroups. Do you have a strong business sense and can teach other moms how to be more efficient with their finances or how to raise money for the group? Perhaps you quietly observe and are intuitive and can help by corresponding with others who need information. There are a host of talents and skills that are needed and can be used in every group.

Your children will make new friends and so will you. You will befriend women who can give you advice on dealing with a myriad of topics. Skilled groups often develop a babysitting plan for a mom's day out and enjoy a cup of coffee, movie or shopping, all without interruption. You get to have time with other adults who need conversation as much as you do. You discover things about yourself that you didn't know. You discuss fun places to visit with the kids, free stuff (and what mom doesn't like that), and referrals for services. In a nutshell, you get as much as you give. Don't be afraid to step out there and meet folks.

WHAT ABOUT COMPATIBILITY ISSUES?

For all the greatness of playgroups, there may be some drawbacks. One such issue could be parenting styles. If you find that you have a style different from the majority of mothers in the group, this could lead to some contention when it comes to children's interactions. How do you handle little Johnny or Alicia hitting your child in the head with a toy bat? Was it accidental or on purpose? Did the other parent notice and what are they going to do about it? All good questions; however, it has to be answered from the perspective of how you parent.

Whether you are self-corrective or strict, you should keep in mind that you are in a group setting, and each child and parent is different and deserves respect, no matter what. The first step is to call your child over and get his take on what happened. Next, you may want to speak to the parent and other child. Get down on the children's level and calmly ask each child what happened. Maybe you missed your child throwing a block at that other child, and this was their retaliation. Either way, both parents should reinforce that this type of behavior is not appropriate for either child and they should each apologize to one another.

If your child needs to find other playmates for a little while, then that is what he should do. However, if the children continue to play together, they must play nicely and respect one another by not doing things that could potentially hurt them, or anyone else. If you notice your child's friend is aggressive, it is your responsibility and option to discontinue or allow that friendship.

Do you stay in the group? Do you talk to the other parent and relay your concerns? Do you talk to the leadership of the group about your concerns and ask them to address the other parent? Do you speak directly to the child? You have to make the right choice for you.

If you value the majority of relationships that get created with other playmates, then choose one of the former options. If you think this child's behavior has soured your playgroup experience, choose one of the middle or later options. Before making any decision, talk to your child (if he is old enough to express a clear thought) and get his take on the situation. Sometimes, you may have to stick it out because he has connected with the group and it is as much an outlet for him as it is for you.

I faced two separate experiences with Jimmy where he was on both sides of the coin. He was both the victim as well as the aggressor. When we were a part of one group, there was one young man Jimmy didn't get along with. It was a great group, and I enjoyed the company of the other mothers; however, every time my son got into the same room with this other child, it was like vinegar and baking soda, always explosive. This boy would taunt Jimmy, hit him, and one time, kicked him and left a bruise.

I did my best to be compassionate and caring towards this kid, but once I saw the bruise, I became "mama bear." I approached the mother of this child and had a talk with her. She said she understood, but this was the only outlet her son had to meet people and make friends. She was struggling to help him control his behavior and didn't know what to do. I told her that I didn't think that the boys should play together for the rest of the day, but I would ponder the situation and get back to her with some possible solutions.

When I next saw her, she said that my suggestions wouldn't work for her family because she didn't believe in stifling her son's energy. I then took it one step further and talked to one of the group's organizers. I simply stated that I would like to know ahead of time if this mother and her son were going to be coming to the playgroup because I had concerns that Jimmy was being mistreated by this child, and I would prefer for them to not play together.

We ultimately stopped going to this playgroup because of that situation. I could have left him in the group and taught him the valuable lesson of how to deal with bullies, but that was not my goal.

Jimmy was three-years-old, and my goal was for him to develop good social skills while having fun. Being bullied was not a part of the "fun" section.

In a separate incident, Jimmy was the aggressive rambunctious child that had to learn to keep his hands to himself. I knew that when Jimmy got excited, all logic flew out the window, and he began to act before he thought. He knew what he should and should not do; however, sometimes he chose to do the wrong thing anyway. We still work on that, even today.

There was a group of boys who were excitable. I allowed Jimmy to play with them. I noticed that in the midst of playing several games, one boy would always come away crying or saying, "Jimmy did this to me." I talked to Jimmy and the other little boy several times before finally deciding to see for myself what was happening. I quietly followed Jimmy and this group of boys. My goal was to become Jimmy's outward conscience. Every time I saw him about to do something harmful to this boy, I made him stop and practice "self-control" so he would consider his actions.

"Self-control" was a form of discipline that I used whereby he had to stand in place without moving for usually 30 seconds or more. This allowed him to gather his thoughts and refocus his energy. It took nearly three play dates, but Jimmy began to think first, then act. He grew an aversion to "self-control" and stopped bullying this boy, and they played well together each time thereafter.

The goal of the playgroup should be twofold: to allow the children to have fun and to allow the parents to enjoy the company of other adults. If you find that you are having problems with another mother, well, that is a bigger issue that needs to be tackled. Sometimes, you may just have to put on your big girl panties and address the concern to the mother herself. You both may have to get over yourselves for the sake of the children. If it is not something you can get over, stop being around that particular group of moms.

There was a mom with whom I shared mutual female friends. We would see each other at different outings. I assumed that because we had a similar group of friends, we would be friends as well. I invited her and her family over for parties, playgroups, and girl-time at my house. I very quickly discovered that my assumption was incorrect. She and I did not connect at all. My main issue centered on how she and her family disrespectfully conducted themselves in my home and at parties. Long story short, I stopped inviting them to our parties and home. We did not do anything beyond seeing each other at other people's events. Our children didn't play together often, so it was no big deal. We were still cordial, but it didn't go any further than that.

Even if you find that your children and another mom's children play well together, you can still be cordial and allow the children to develop a friendship. Hopefully, you and the other mom will come to a place where you can at least appreciate each other for being moms and for the fact that your children enjoy each other's company.

Last year, I joined a playgroup where all the women were really great and our children all played well together. However, I didn't click with the moms, and my children didn't develop friendships with their children. We continued to attend the group because the meeting time was convenient. They did things outside of the playgroup that I chose not to attend. I think I missed out on opportunities to get to know those women on a deeper, more meaningful level because my ill-founded perception was based in some obscure intangible thing that was lacking. It was a regret that I had, but a lesson learned.

Going forward, I know, I have to make the effort to get to know moms on a new more expansive level before discounting the connection. I have to put on my big girl panties and move my ego out of the picture.

> *"Friendship is born at the moment when one person says to another, 'What! You too? I thought I was the only one."*
>
> – C.S. Lewis

NOTES:

Chapter 6

Do What I Say Child

"Human beings are the only creatures that allow their children to come back home."
— Bill Cosby

Why is it that at some point in our journey of mommy-hood, we find ourselves saying, "Just do what I say, because I say so!" Even moms-in-training who have only babysat a child have thought it or said it out loud. I remember, as a child, I would hate it when my mother uttered those famous words. I wanted to question her, but I think I would have seen next week way too early! Instead, I made the internal declaration, "When I grow up and become a mom, I'm never going to say that." I've broken that declaration plenty of times. However, I explained some things to my children and didn't just end up with a "because I said so." To ease my conscience and make me feel a tad better, I did live up to a part of that declaration.

There are times when a parent has the right to say it, and it has to be enough with no explanation necessary. It could be a life-or-death situation, or where a child needs to act quickly. Sometimes, it's too late, you're tired, and your child wants to challenge you by playing 20 questions instead of going to bed on time. Whatever the reason, use this phrase sparingly.

As a parent, have you violated any of those oh-so-pervasive statements that used to irritate us as children? What about, "Do what I say and not what I do?" "When I was a child, my mother used to make me _____." "You don't know how lucky you are. Out there is a child that doesn't have ¼ of what you have. Yet you complain" (used this one last week)! "When I was your age, _____."

Sometimes, I feel like I have turned into my mother...not that this is such a bad thing. It's funny to think that the things she and my grandmother would say I am now saying on a regular basis. I swore to myself I would never do it, but here I am doing it constantly! I guess there is wisdom in aging or in repetition that I never embraced until now. I also see that I am a product of what I was told and the examples of what I was shown.

In spite of my many declarations, I still manage to have those words ingrained in my mind so I can't help but say them. I reflect on the importance of words and how crucial it is that we, as moms, plant good words into our children's hearts. Once words are spoken, you can't take them back. You have to replace them with something reaffirming and do it until the child really grabs a hold of it and embraces the new thought.

A little while ago, a crushing thing happened that made me analyze myself and reminded me not to speak flippantly without understanding the repercussions. One school morning, we were feeling rushed, or let me say I was feeling rushed. Jimmy was taking his time playing with the water, his shoelaces, his toys, and doing everything he could to not get dressed. I yelled up to him, and he finally came down after about 40 minutes.

After playing all morning, he appears from around the corner with his school uniform on (red shirt and navy pants) and has white socks pulled up to his knees on top of his pants. He had his black sneakers on with his undershirt stretched up covering the back of his head. I looked at him and blurted out, "You look like the village idiot."

OK, not one of my proudest moments, and words I dearly regret. As I turned around to finish making their lunches, I heard the soft sounds of sniffling and turned around to see my boy with his head hung low. The tears rolled down his cheeks and on his face was the saddest most pitiful look he could muster. I stopped what I was doing and walked to where he was and gave him a big hug. "Jimmy, I'm sorry for what I said."

"Mom, you called me an idiot. We're not allowed to use that word."

Instantly, my heart sank in my chest and a big lump welled up in my throat. I wanted to cry. I started out by saying, "NO, I wasn't saying you are an idiot. I was referring to a character called…" I stopped and said, "I'm sorry. I never meant to call you an idiot. That is not a good word, and I will never use it again. Can you please forgive me?"

He said he forgave me, but the look on his face said he was still wrestling with my words. I apologized again and said, "You are the most intelligent boy I know. You are an amazing son and brother who is super smart, sweet and kindhearted. You achieve everything you put your mind to. All your friends love being around you, and most importantly, I love you so much. I didn't mean to hurt you and because I did, I am sorry." After I said those things, the tears stopped flowing and his countenance changed. I hugged him and again affirmed my love. Again, he forgave me.

It was a lesson learned and one that will not soon be repeated. I'm well aware of the impact of my words. In that moment of frustration and jest, I forgot how quickly my words could cut to the heart of my child. You're probably wondering why in the heck someone who can be so careless with words is writing a book. Well, it was a temporary lapse. To all those moms out there who mess up occasionally, or don't always get it right, I identify and place myself among you.

I use my mistakes and triumphs to illustrate a point about my humanity and learning from challenges, too. Every challenge is not only about your child, it is about you. How will you respond to what comes your way? How do you handle the hectic morning routine with managing to be sane through it all? Moms go through a lot, and whatever situation arises, we need to learn from it so that it is not repeated. Are you a big enough woman to acknowledge and apologize for your mistakes and allow your child to see that you are human too? Will you model the best behavior you can in order to show your child that you mean what you say and say what you mean?

I found out that even though I feel like what I say goes in one ear and out the other my children cling to every word I say. Sometimes they may not actively listen, but they hear me. I think that it depends on the processing capabilities of each child. Some children, like Victoria, are quick to listen, hear and do. While others, like Jimmy, listen, hear, and need some time to marinate on what is said before actually doing it. Do you ever find yourself in the midst of rushing and allow comments to fly out of your mouth? I am hopeful you will learn to stop, then speak more carefully.

Keep in mind that through the process of creating a vision and plan for your life and the lives of your children, you have to be a positive example. This is a journey for you to become the mom you want to be so you can then positively affect the person you want your child to become. This may sound ominous and unattainable. It won't be, if you keep working to ensure you think before you speak and don't allow the situations around you to determine the environment you create with your words.

There is a show on PBS called *Word World*. I love this show because it teaches children how to spell and join word sounds. It solidifies the idea that children can use their words to create the world around them. It is profound and yet simple. Everything is made up of words. The words we speak create the environment in which we live. Some spoken words don't manifest in our environment until later, while others affect us immediately. Ultimately, if we understand the power of words, we will begin to speak things that are important and weighted and create a positive world in which to live.

Have you ever felt something coming on and said, "Uh-oh, I think a cold is coming on," and within a day or so, you have a full-blown cold that is wreaking havoc on your life? What about telling your child, "Sit in the chair instead of standing because you might fall off," and then they fall? Victoria told me that she wanted a baby brother, and then a baby sister. Within a few months of her pronouncement, I was pregnant with the gender of the child SHE said she wanted.

Truthfully, our words do frame our world and it is up to us whether we frame them positively or negatively. Even if we have the best intentions in the world, they amount to nothing if all we do is speak harshly or negatively. Some children have the temperament to soak it all up and use it as fuel to succeed and prove they are not the negative things that were said about them. Other children get crushed under the weight of the words and can resort to either lashing out because they are fulfilling the label that was placed on them, or they allow others to abuse them (verbally, mentally, physically, or emotionally). Others simply may cower and never succeed to their potential because they are weighted down by the stigma that they cannot do it.

I never want to look back on my life and think I handicapped my children by hampering their potential. Potential is the fuel that makes boys and girls grow up to be great adults. Do you know your child's personality quirks? Can you focus on them in a positive way?

One year, I had a situation with Victoria in school where she hated to read out loud because she got nervous. Some of the kids made fun of her for being so quiet. Despite being an above-average reader for her class, she got stage fright. Victoria's personality is very demure at times, and she is very sensitive, yet passionate about doing well and succeeding. One day, I noticed she was reading very loudly when she thought no one was paying attention. When I began listening to her, she became very quiet. To help her shyness, we had her read aloud in front of family members every day.

Our goal was to take her desire to succeed and transpose it over her shyness so that she would overcome this issue. I then asked her teacher to e-mail me a note updating me on Victoria's progress in class. When we received her teacher's correspondence, Victoria smiled and was so happy to hear that her teacher thought she was doing an excellent job and wanted her to read more in class. As her mom, my job was to observe and assess her need (again, COO of Personnel Development and Operations). I figured out the best way to present the information to Victoria so she could excel.

You have to get to know your children and how they receive information. If you don't learn their personalities, how they learn, or what motivates them, you will find it very difficult in later years to do those things. The great teenage divide might be the result.

> *"As you ramble on through life, my brother, Whatever be your goal, Keep your eye upon the doughnut and not upon the hole."*
>
> Zoltan Gottlieb

NOTES:

Chapter 7

CAN I SKIP WHAT YOU JUST SAID?

"A ship is safe in harbor, but that's not what ships are for."

– William Shedd

We just discussed how what you say is important, but in my experience, what is NOT said is just as important, and sometimes more. I remember being a child and going to stay with my southern relatives for summer vacation. There were a couple of times where I was told, "A child is seen and not heard. Stay out of grown folks' business!"

It was as if I had no right to exist when there were adults around and they were talking. Oddly, there were certain conversations that I overheard or things I had seen that were definitely not appropriate for a child's ears and eyes. They affected me as much as being told that I was to stay out of grown folks' business.

Inwardly, I wanted to know that when I talked, I was heard and what I said was valued. By being told that I was to be seen and not heard, I was made to feel like I had no value and was not important. Because of this unsaid subtext I became a very pensive and shy child. Instead of talking a lot, I learned to watch and observe people. I watched the very people who said these things to me, and I learned that what they said and what they did were totally different.

Subtext means a lot to a child, and if things are not explained, children are left to their own imaginations. Think of explaining how babies are born. OK, don't hyperventilate if you haven't had this talk yet. If young children hear someone say the stork dropped the baby off, they might believe them. Mentally, they connect seeing the picture of the stork with the baby in the blanket and it makes sense, even though Mom and Dad never fully explained.

As children grow and mature, they connect the dots. They realize that Mommy's tummy was big, now it isn't. Mommy is in the hospital, and they have a new little brother or sister. They know the stork thing isn't fully correct, so they question more and you give vague, yet truthful answers.

We described childbirth in comparison to fruit ripening and flowers blooming. I had a seed in my tummy, and when the time was right, the seed began to grow into a baby. When the baby got big enough, he or she had to come out. I explained further that I had to go to the hospital so the doctors could help get the baby out of my tummy. The machines were there to make sure mommy and baby were both safe. Our children understood the commonalities and there were fewer breaks in the chain. They were filling in the blanks until they matured enough to ask more sound questions and have the process explained.

Hearing children fill in the blanks can be amusing. If you ask them basic questions, you will hear how often they make up their own answers when they don't know the real answers. As a fun example, ask your children these questions and listen to the answers, but don't laugh out loud.

What do you think I was like as a child?
What do I do when you're not around?
What am I really good at?
What do I do for a job?
What am I not good at?
How are you and I different?
Who is the boss in our house?
What would it take to make me perfect?
Where does money come from?

I hope you wrote down the answers. Date it and make sure to keep track of it over the upcoming years. When your children get older, everyone will enjoy the innocence of their responses. If you really want unbiased answers, get another person to ask your child these questions about you.

Now that you have had a good laugh, what do you think about what just happened? What message have you sent to your child about who you are?

I know, deep and heavy for such simple questions, but we have to learn to see through the eyes of our children. Victoria once told me that she thought I went through a phase where I was angry all the time. Even though she wasn't sure, my voice seemed tense and it wasn't fun for a little while.

I was surprised, but had to realize this was my child's perception, and a valid one. Perception is reality, and who we are is not always defined by the sweet core of humanity tied up in each of us. It is how we present ourselves to others. Sometimes, *what* we say gets muddled beneath *how* we say things. There is a difference between our normal tone and our "mommy tone of voice." The "mommy tone of voice" generally means that we are serious and that fun and games are over. I guess I had my "mommy voice" on so often that I forgot what my normal voice sounded like. I am more aware of my tone now and can easily turn it off and on when needed.

The time Victoria referred to was particularly challenging because I was under tremendous stress navigating a large state to state move; being delicate and understanding of the children's feelings about the move; having James slightly stressed about how to effectively and cautiously leave his job for a new one; selling our home while finding a new one; and still maintaining the daily chores and activities.

It was challenging to look deeper into the disparity between who I thought I was and others' perceptions of me. My daughter's observation of me helped me to bridge the gap between those two thoughts. I had this ideal that I was taking it all in stride. That was obviously a figment of my imagination, like the times I could survive off of four hours of sleep and two double shots of espresso, then run all day, and literally be every woman. Unfortunately, that chick doesn't live HERE anymore! I can no longer be her, even when I work hard at it. I look exhausted because I am overwhelmed.

A few months ago, I was remembering the glory days of my twenties where I pulled all-nighters and thought I could still do it. I sabotaged myself because I didn't get anything of substance completed during the normal day. So, without thinking, I stayed up all night doing chores while I played on the internet. The next morning, I gulped coffee to stay awake until I could get the kids ready for breakfast and school.

I barely made it to 9am before I crashed on the floor. It innocently began as watching television with Ella. It turned ugly when she decided to play by jumping her 26 pound body on my back. I was jolted awake and shocked that I didn't realize I had fallen asleep. Thankfully my mom lives with us and was able to watch Ella while I slept and recouped. For me, I know I am not every woman and she does not live inside of me. I am no longer the vibrant 20-something who could stay awake all night. I guess that was my reality check, and I have morphed into a seasoned mom.

If you are that mom who is always running and barely stops, I invite you to think of how you can streamline everyone's activities and other priorities that steal your time. Find a way to make memories that don't sap your energy, enthusiasm, and joy out of being a mom.

All I can say is to choose wisely who you want to be and let that be the message you communicate to those around you. Remember, what you say and how you say things are also important. Just as important are the subconscious thoughts that play out in our expressions, tones of voice, behavior, and reactions to different situations.

DON'T YOU KNOW I LOVE YOU?

"Baby, you know I love you."
"If you do, then tell me."

I often assume that my children and family know that I love them by all the things I do and have given up for them. I assume that my love is somehow transmitted through some neon flashing sign above my head when I put dinner on the table, do laundry, pick them up from school, or have lunch with them. Yes, all of these things do send a message of love, but if I never say it, I leave a gaping hole that will be filled by someone other than me.

Now, let's turn the tables and put you in the following scenario. You are a mom who gets up early so you can get yourself ready for the day. You prepare your children's breakfast, pack lunch, and make sure the kids are awake. If you are a working mom, you work all day. Stay-at-home-moms do all the housework and personal chores. A vast part of the population are moms in higher education and have that dynamic to contend with. I salute any mom who is any combination of the above.

If the children are in extracurricular activities, there is a whole block of time that gets eaten up in the afternoon. You finish with your day of work and are now home with the children. You have wearily helped with homework as you prepared dinner and got ready to end the evening. The night ends with you finally cleaning up the house and heading off to bed.

If you do this day-in and day-out without so much as a "thank you, Mom" or "I love you Mom," how would you feel? I think I can confidently say that any mom would be upset. You might even harbor feelings of resentment at the situation. If you are married or have a significant other, and he neither helped nor acknowledged your monumental efforts, you would feel even worse.

I walked the dog on this example so that you would have an understanding of how it feels to not have a vocal expression of appreciation. Your children need directed and personalized affirmations. They need to know and hear that they are loved and appreciated simply because they exist. I'm not talking about a hokey or obligatory "I love you kid," but a sincere heartfelt effective conveyance of emotion.

Speaking directly to your child instead of in a passing moment will help personalize your statements. It also means complimenting them on what they did right and telling them how and why they did it right. This helps focus your sentiments as personal and tangible. Instead of linking praise to an action, make it more of a character infusion.

When Jimmy or Victoria set the table for dinner, my response is focused on them being thoughtful to me and the family by doing something that helps everyone. I highlight what they did, as part of them knowing that thoughtfulness is a valuable and appreciated character trait.

Regardless of the grades they receive in school, I always inquire about their effort. Our focus is to reward the effort and teach the children the difference between a lackadaisical effort and one that is truly their best. Children know when they give something their all and when they half step.

You will learn to decipher between a good and a great effort when you watch them in different settings. Watch them when they are doing homework that may be difficult for them. Note when they are doing something they enjoy (sports or hobbies) where they want to win.

If they give it their all and still do not come out on top, it teaches them persistence. Just make sure that your tone and your words are inspirational and not condemning. Inspire them to persist and reach their greatest heights. Tell a personal story or find another story or two to reaffirm how persistence will ultimately lead to victory. Acknowledge that you understand it is difficult for them, but you know they can stick with it and do it! The point is to focus on specific, direct, and personal actions that lead to building up a great character in your child.

Your children need to know that you love them and that's why you can't skip over using positive, uplifting words. You can't tell them to do as you say and not what you do. Explain things in terms that are age-appropriate and don't leave them to their own imaginations. Have a plan to model the example you wish for them to follow and ensure you are making memories that last a lifetime.

You are the mom who can make it all possible by not burning yourself out. You have creative power and compassion towards your children. You exhibit control while infusing expectations that help your children grow. Your hugs and kisses soothe all hurts. You are one of a kind! After all, you are the greatest mom in the whole wide world for your child!

"It always seems impossible until it's done."
— Nelson Mandela

Laundry Can Wait

NOTES:

PART 2

TAKING A MINUTE FOR YOU

CHAPTER 8

BRING SEXY BACK!!

"Confidence is the sexiest thing a woman can have. It's much sexier than any body part."
– Aimee Mullins

Woman

Part one focused on our roles as moms and why it's important to have a vision for our lives. Now it's time to take a few minutes to talk about us as: a woman first, wives second, and mothers third. For anyone who wants to take the freeway approach, I'm sorry, but we're going to be taking the scenic route with this one. This is probably the most pivotal and important section of this book.

We often get our roles out of order by allowing our motherhood to trump being a woman or a wife! That is like having a scale and putting a small can of beans on one side, and putting a commercial sized can of the same beans on the other and then wondering why they aren't equal. We put so much weight on being a mother that we forget the essence of what we are made of, and that's, uniquely, woman.

Before you were a wife or mother, you were a woman. Did you identify yourself as strong, confident, athletic, focused, independent, assertive, professional, or determined to achieve certain goals in your life? Maybe you were an artist, musician, dancer, or creative type. Were you free spirited, easygoing, or very relaxed? Perhaps you were a combination. We leave the important role of "woman," in lieu of another. We bankrupt ourselves with the daily work of taking care of others. You might still be the woman you were BMAC (before marriage and children). If you are, that is truly incredible and amazing. I want to hear from you on the blog! If you are like many of us, at one point in your child rearing or marriage, you lost sight of who you were.

I must confess that between three and five years of marriage and kids number one and two, I was out of balance and resembled someone I didn't recognize. The outer shell of Dorothy was there for all to see, but I was missing a big part. I was on autopilot. I merely existed from day-to-day and floated between things-to-do. I was content, but not happy; full, but not fulfilled; and busy, but not accomplished. This was not a reflection of my husband or children, but more a reflection of me. I had forgotten who I was and wallowed in the self-pity of my forgotten dreams.

I had dreams of being a corporate executive and owning several businesses that all worked together. I wanted to write a book or two about anything. I envisioned owning a shopping center with a daycare so I could have my children nearby while I ran my business next door. I imagined being debt-free and having a net worth of over three-to-five million dollars. I wanted quite a lot, yet had not done any of what I had imagined. I was still myself with all my hopes and dreams buried inside of me, but none of them were ready to be born.

I opted to focus on motherhood instead. Like many, I perceived I had to choose between my dreams or my children. All too often, we suffer as a consequence. The silver lining is that our dreams do not have to take a back seat to our roles. We can achieve all that we desire out of life. It won't be easy, but hard work never is.

Are you willing to temporarily sacrifice for your dreams and what are you willing to give up? Would you give up watching hours of television or surfing the internet mindlessly? Can you sleep a little less to get more work done? If you can answer yes, then figure out what is it you want to do and how soon. Having a set goal and planning time for your vision is pivotal to making it a reality. If you need a refresher on the realities of goal setting, go back to chapter 1 and review the top 10 reasons why people don't achieve their goals. Choose to not be one of those people, and then start writing.

Several mothers I know have made the conscience decision to set high goals, attend to their families, and find time for themselves. I often marvel at how they juggle it all in the midst of perceived chaos. From what I understand, the solace is in knowing that many of their sacrifices are temporary and meant to better the lives of themselves and their families.

Cynthia is one of the hardest-working women I know. She has two children (aged four and six years old) and is in the process of getting her master's degree. Her husband is an attorney with the United Nations and is frequently gone for months at a time. I cannot imagine the stress that is created by having to work 40 hours during the weekend, going to graduate school and working two part-time jobs during the week, attending karate or soccer practices and meets, along with being a full time dual-role parent. In spite of all of her hard work, her children are extremely well-rounded, and have the greatest personalities. Her relationship with them continually evolves. Cynthia also manages to make time to see her girlfriends and family members.

Yolanda was a single mother raising a teenage son. She is a professor of mathematics as well as a writer of math textbooks. She is an accomplished woman who takes life by the horns and steers it in the direction she wants it to go. She has single-handedly raised her son to be diligent and goal oriented. She has always worked hard to provide for her and her son. Her son recently received a four-year scholarship to a prestigious university with a guaranteed job upon graduation. Yolanda has done a tremendous job because she realizes the importance of personal time. She loves going to the spa, working out, and having time for herself.

Marie is another very hardworking mother. Marie has three children (aged four, seven, and 15 years old), is in a master's degree program with a required internship, and is planning to do the Ph.D. program immediately afterwards. Marie has always pushed herself to succeed. Like Cynthia, Marie loses sleep and has to be in several places at once, but those are some of the sacrifices she has made so that she can remain true to herself and her goals as a woman. She manages to find time for herself in the midst of her children's games, school or church plays, and church choir. The most impressive thing, above all, is that she finds time once a week to catch up with friends for lunch.

Tammy is a college math professor, pastor for youth and teens, and an amazing teacher of the Word of God. Tammy and her husband, Jeff, have four beautiful children (three girls and one boy). Tammy is extremely creative, occasionally teaches dance classes, and loves to help youth and teens. She is so precious and whenever she laughs, you not only know she's in the room, you laugh and smile, and your heart fills with love. Never have I met someone who so willingly gives of herself, yet works adamantly to preserve her identity as a woman, wife, mother, teacher, and friend. We often joke about one of her special interests as an herbal and all-natural guru. If you ever need information on home remedies, herbal substitutes, or organic foods, just ask and she willingly tells all she knows. Tammy is a great friend and an example for all who come into her sphere of influence.

Kelli is a stay-at-home-mom, has four lovely children (three boys and one girl) ranging in age from toddler to teen. She is also a women's pastor, the leader of an incredible young women's group in Arizona (over 300 members) and co-leader with her husband Jason (also an international Christian recording artist and lead singer of Re:Zound) of a fantastic young couples' group. Kelli's children are wonderful dancers and musicians and she finds time to help in their classrooms. She is an avid scrap booker and teacher of God's Word. I don't know everything she does from day-to-day or what her children do, but I wish I had her strength and energy. Somehow Kelli still finds time to read, do her hobby, and spend time with her close friends and family.

Kristin is a stay-at-home-mom extraordinaire! She has four children (two boys and two girls), all under the age of eight-years-old. She is amazing in that she adjusts to anything thrown her way. When her toddler Kyler practiced his pitching arm by seeing how far raw eggs would go, she smiled, took pictures and put them on her family's blog. Every summer, Kristin hosts a back-to-school sleepover for her daughters and six to ten of their closest friends. Every girl leaves her house on cloud nine with a CD of over 100 pictures. When I say, "over-the-top experience," I mean it with love. She is naturally creative and invests her love, time, and energy into all that she does. She is an amazing seamstress for her home, and she even has time for her business, *Pampered Tots Boutique*, where she channels all her unique talents. She is an amazing friend whose words inspire, photos enlighten, and whom everyone loves. Did I mention her house is pristine all the time and she has four kids under eight-years-old? I don't know how she does it, but man, I wish I knew!

There are many women that I admire, but these women stand out. They juggle their lives yet are balanced in spending time with their families. I esteem them for all they are able to accomplish in lines with their goals and dreams. Their families are not picture perfect with no problems or issues. Heck, we're all human and have some sort of issue, but the important thing is that these women work through them and do what needs to be done for the greater good of their family.

The lady who does not forget that she is a woman first is going to be the most successful woman of all. She will always be fulfilled. I almost sound like a fortune cookie, but in this case, it's not a fortune, but practical wisdom.

BRINGING SEXY BACK - WOMAN

Part of being a sexy woman is learning that you are gorgeous and full of life. Sexiness is an attitude more so than a look or the clothes you put on, although certain clothes inherently make you feel sexy. *Bringing Sexy Back* is about updating your mind to have a positive self-image. It does not matter if you are a size 0 or a size 24; sexiness is about you and how you see yourself. Whether you are curvaceous or have a muffin top and cottage cheese, learn to love every part of you. Those physical attributes can be changed and are not the total package of you.

As a sexy woman, you have to shed all those false mental constructs of what you should look like and how you should act. For goodness sake, stop enviously comparing yourself to other women. You should have a role model who pushes you forward, but realize she is human and has flaws. You are uniquely and divinely YOU, created to be amazing, and achieve greatness. You are filled with love and have so much love to give. When you learn to truly love and appreciate yourself, you will stop abusing yourself.

You abuse yourself by giving to everyone else and saving nothing for you. It is not selfish to save for yourself, so get that crazy thought out of your mind. Selfish is when you think of yourself only and no one else. Selfless is when you think of everyone and never yourself. Women, stop putting yourselves at the bottom or leaving yourself off of your list. Make a point to do something every day for yourself. If it's just drinking a cup of coffee or tea, having meditation time, reading, or some hobby, do it. It recharges you and allows you time to decompress so you have energy to give to others.

I like comparing women to banks. Banks are rich in resources and abundantly full of what others need. If others withdraw money from the bank and never make a deposit, the bank will soon be bankrupt and have nothing to give. We are like the bank. If we always give without making a deposit, we will soon be mentally and spiritually bankrupt. This is where I was when I spoke earlier about being the shell of myself. I didn't understand balance and had no idea that I was not giving to myself. I had no idea that I needed to regenerate and recoup.

Before I got married, I was the picture of a modern woman who knew what she wanted out of life and profession. I carried my briefcase and wore my suits with confidence and poise. By years three to five of marriage, my mind still thought professionally, but all else was left behind. I was confused with the direction my life was headed. I only had one or two close confidants and felt lonely because I couldn't fully express all that was going on internally. I was overwhelmed as I barely managed existing. It was easier to not have to deal with me, so I focused on my children and husband. I got good at it. So good that I didn't realize I needed an outlet for me until year six of marriage.

I did not realize how unwrapped I was until I went on my first girls trip. It was then that a whole new world opened to me and I understood decompression and time away from the family. At first, I thought the trip was selfish. I could not understand why some of my friends wanted to go away without our kids and husbands. I was enlightened and learned that going away allowed all of us time to miss and appreciate all that I do as a mom and wife. I rediscovered who I was, and I got in touch with ME! I came back refreshed, revived, and ready to tackle my role in a new way. I was inspired to be better. You need to carve out some time to focus on you, the woman, first and foremost.

The external part of bringing sexy back as a woman is finding clothing that compliments and makes you feel sexy and confident. One of my sexiest outfits is a pair of black low-rise jeans, spaghetti strap balloon bottom shirt, and black four-inch heels. That outfit makes me feel absolutely unstoppable! When I wear it, I feel like everyone is looking at me saying, "I want to look like THAT!" OK, well, not so much, but it makes me feel like a woman and not a "mommy."

I've got plenty of "mommy" clothes, but when James and I go out on a date, I put on my "grown up" clothes and imagine that we are dating BMAC. Something else I do is leave Ella at the daycare or with my mother and I get my hair done. It's a treat that I reserve for special occasions, but if you can do it more often, you should. I also like to get a manicure and pedicure or massage and spa treatment. It is not always possible to go often, but I make a point to do beautification. When I can't get a massage or mani-pedicure I beg my family for help. I have taught my children and husband how to do different massage techniques.

If you do not have the financial resources, there are plenty of other things you can do. It may require more work, but you get the same result. If you have a cosmetology school near where you live, find out when they accept live models. You can normally get your hair done for under $20 and nails done for a fraction of that. Massage schools, may need live bodies to work on too! There are plenty of creative ways to relax. If you do not have any of these schools near you, set aside time to do it yourself, or get a good friend to help you do your hair and nails.

I have learned to relax and feel great about myself from the inside out. Because of that, when I focus on the outside, I can't but help to feel sexy. Find something that you can do or wear that helps to bring the sexy woman out of you. You deserve it, and you need to start depositing back into you so you can help others to the best of your abilities.

WIFE

I love my role as a wife and enjoy being married to my husband, but I realize that it is another role to fulfill. This relationship is the key to the family; I think it's worth some time to delve into the female perspective of how this works.

One pivotal part of being a wife is meant to maintain the love between you and your husband. You have to keep the lines of communication open so that nothing can come in between the two of you. It also means taking time out of your life and getting involved in the life of your husband. You can't reserve all of your attention and love for the children and forget the man who helped you to create them.

It's interesting because the first year and a half of marriage before Victoria was born, I dedicated the majority of my time and energy to James. I didn't exclude my friends or go into seclusion; I learned to make him one of my best friends. We'd enjoy quiet nights, game nights, nonstop fun nights, and nights full of any and everything that we wanted to do. I looked forward to it and relished in every moment. We would sit down annually to create a plan of our future goals. We were in tune with each other, and it was a blissful post-honeymoon.

Contrast that with the first year of marriage as a threesome with a brand new baby. I was too tired to do anything remotely related to fun. I found that all my free time was now spent taking care of Victoria. I was always tired, and when I wasn't tired, I spent time with James and some time with Victoria. I allowed myself to be totally consumed with being a mother that I forgot how to be a wife. Poor James was left to fend for himself and expected to give more than a Herculean effort around the house. He had to take care of the real estate office before coming home and eating franks and beans because that's all I had time to make. Thank goodness I have progressed to making full meals now.

Yes, it was important that I devoted crucial time to my new baby. I had to learn what being a mother was about as there was undoubtedly a learning curve. No one will ever fault a mother for caring for her child. However, the word balance is where we have to learn to navigate towards.

Before we were moms, we were in a loving relationship, and we can't forget that we have to nurture that relationship. When the children are on their way out the door to chart their life path, what will your life amass to, and what type of relationship will you and your spouse garner? I want to know that, as my children grow, they are exposed to a loving example of what a marriage is meant to produce.

I am cognizant of the example that we are setting for our children. Children will more than likely mimic the relationships they see, and I want that relationship to be amazing. I want my daughters to know that they are queens who should be treated with the highest level of respect, love, and esteem. I want my son to see that he is a king who provides and protects, while having a strong and confident wife able to love him and take care of the family. I want my children to experience partnership to the fullest extent. This is what James and I consistently attempt to model.

Growing up in a single-parent household, I did not see the "couple" relationship. All I had were shows like: *The Cosby Show, The Brady Bunch, Little House on the Prairie, The Partridge Family and Family Ties*. I looked at their families and wanted what they had. I wanted a mom and a dad who were fun and loving, plus baked cookies. I desired my mom to be home when I got out of school. What I wanted and what I had were two different things.

My mother pulled double-duty as mother and father. She worked all day, then came home and made dinner for five children. She was continually burned out. She tried to have time for herself, but ultimately, we would often compete for her limited attention. She managed to provide each of us with all that was in her, but she often neglected herself.

Although I used the *Cosby Show* as the precursor for my "ideal life," I used my mother as the reality check. What I took from my early years centered on developing characteristics that have helped me succeed. I learned how to be doggedly determined to not accept less than my best. I purposed to do anything I set my mind to. I recognized that women are the strongest creatures on the planet. I also understood that a mother never stops until her children are provided for. My mother's and grandmother's examples of devotion were the basis for many of my perceptions.

As an encouragement to single mothers, just hang on. Your efforts are not in vain! Your children will one day be able to help you, allowing you time for yourself. You are doing such an amazing job, and what you are pouring into the lives of your children is helping them to model the characteristics that will make their lives a success.

As women, we sometimes miss that our children are watching us to see how we are as women. They want to see that we are taking time for ourselves. They need us to show them what behavior they should model, very similar to children playing 'house' or 'teacher.' We have to provide a positive example from which to draw. If you are single, focus on character traits and be the best woman and mother you can be. If you are married, model that relationship and do it to the best of your ability.

James and I choose to represent the loving and intimate part of our relationship. When he comes home and greets me with a kiss, immediately the girls follow up with, "Daddy, kiss me too. Kiss, Daddy." They want to get the same affection that mom is receiving. When Jimmy sees us kiss, he starts laughing and says, "Yuck," yet he also wants one from James and me. James and I hug, and the kids all smile, and make that funny "eww" sound to show their fake displeasure.

We know that our displays of affection let our children know we are in love and they can be secure in that fact. We tastefully kiss and hug in front of the children so they can learn that affection is a good thing, meant to happen between a man and woman in a loving relationship. We want them to expect to love and be loved by showing it.

BRINGING SEXY BACK - WIFE

When you and your spouse first dated, I'm sure you used to dress up and make yourself look amazing. Now that you have won the guy and maybe had a child or two, it doesn't mean you shouldn't do the same anymore. If you don't already do it, make dating your spouse at least monthly, a requirement. Talk about movies, politics, anything (minimize the kid talk though)! Make sure to keep the fires of romance burning so that once the children leave the house and it's you and your husband, you don't wake up one morning realizing you are married, yet you are strangers.

Considering recent surveys and a multitude of blog sites dedicated to divorce, coupled with show topics on both *Oprah* and *The View*, there has been a considerable increase in divorces with those who have been married for 20 and 30 years. All report that over time, couples lose connection with one another because they are so focused on raising their children, working to support the family, and dealing with the daily activities of living, that they disconnect from each other. WWW.divorcerate.org, credits some staggering statistics of a cumulative of 50% of all marriages will end in divorce. The site also shows a 60-74% divorce rate for those embarking on their second or third marriages.

Mature couples may have poured so much into living life that they forgot to pour into each other. WWW.divorcepeers.com credits 21% of divorces to "growing apart," 16% to "falling out of love," and 13% "argued constantly." Having read about or seen this many times in people we met, James and I vowed to not fall prey to these statistics. In our monthly dating, we may have a cup of coffee outside the house or go grocery shopping without the kids. Other times, we do more diverse things like comedy or jazz shows. Whatever the activity, we make time to share in each other's lives so we always stay connected.

Our journey towards this point began when Victoria was about eight months old. She was finally sleeping in her own room and the revelation that if we didn't work towards continually renewing the fires of love, James and I would be in a miserable place. I chose to stop being tired, or rather disinterested in anything that was not Victoria-related. I reminded myself that I had a husband who loved me, wanted me, and needed some personal time and affection. I would pick out the most flattering outfit I could find and we'd go out. If we couldn't find a sitter, we would take Victoria with us, but when we got home, we would put her to bed early so that we could spend time uninterrupted. The point has always been to work with what we had and enjoy each other.

Now that we have three children, the dynamics of planning has changed. When James and I make a plan to spend either a night or a weekend away from the house, these crazy kids automatically assume they are going with us. We quickly halt that choo-choo train! Once they find out that they are not going, they start whining and giving us puppy dog eyes. "Why can't we come? It's not fair that only you and

Daddy get to go to the hotel. We want to come, too." James and I laugh and tell them, "Mommy and Daddy need adult time without the kids. Husbands and wives need time apart from their children."

To make the transition easier, hire a sitter for the night, ask family members or close friends to watch the kids, or set up a sleepover for the kids at a friend's house. Whatever it takes to spend time with your spouse, do it!

Ladies, don't underestimate the power of romance. Squirt his favorite perfume on top of a negligee. Put on his favorite music and top the scene off with pleasing aromas. Sometimes, you may not have that much time, so don't forget about the spur-of-the-moment 'quickie.' Whatever you can do to create a passionate mood for your spouse, feel free to enjoy it. Being a wife means you are sometimes responsible for loving and serving your husband. No, I don't mean in a third-century sense. I mean finding out what he enjoys and what makes him feel loved and then doing it. This is neither a license nor a command to do something that you do not feel comfortable doing. It is simply meant to say that you should not be totally complacent in the bedroom, always waiting for your husband to initiate lovemaking.

That's all I'm going to say on that! You get the idea, so no need to draw the map. I will say that as wives, we need to broaden our idea of what romance entails. Loving your spouse starts the minute you wake up and doesn't end until you both go to sleep at night. Love is a choice to shower your spouse with words of encouragement. When was the last time you told your spouse you were proud of him? When was the last time you slipped a note into his workbag letting him know you love him and are glad he is a part of your life? When was the last time you told your husband he "completes you?" (OK, sorry, I had to slip in a *Jerry McGuire* moment.) When you affirm your admiration and appreciation for your spouse, you convey love to him. In turn, he will love you how you need to be loved.

Bringing sexy back as a wife is something that has to be done continually. It is not a quick fix but rather a lifetime of learning to love and evolve in that love. In the midst of being a wife, don't forget that you are your husband's cheerleader. As a cheerleader, you can encourage and motivate your husband like no one else. When you meet his need for appreciation, acceptance, respect, and love, he will certainly meet all your needs for support, strength, communication, adoration, and love. I invite you to think of new and creative ways to bring sexy back and love on your man!

MOTHER

As women, we can do so much and take on so many things. Mothers inherently can do ten different things at once. I read the cutest e-mail a few months back about how mothers have C.I.A.D.D. (Child Induced Attention Deficit Disorder). A mother starts the day by running the dishwasher and then starts to take out the trash. The phone rings, so she puts the trash down to talk for a few minutes while she makes breakfast. After she hangs up, she calls the children down for breakfast. After breakfast she realizes the trash needs to be taken out, so she starts heading to the door only to realize the kids are about to be late. She takes the kids to school and then returns home. She realizes she needs groceries, so she heads to the grocery store without her list but tries to remember everything. She gets home and realizes she was supposed to pick up the dry cleaning. She says she'll get it when she gets the kids from school. She starts to make lunch, and then realizes she needs to get the car washed. She starts washing the car, and realizes she has to get the kids from school. She starts dinner and does a load of laundry, only to realize that the trash is still sitting there, she forgot to pick up the laundry, the car is still dirty, there is still a load of laundry in the washer, and she never ate lunch. Wondering why she feels so tired and got little done, she just collapses in bed and says, "Tomorrow is another day."

Some days I feel like I am running from one task to another, yet I feel like I started 20 projects and completed none. On other days, the cape is peeking out from my jogging suit, and I have the big "SM" (SuperMom) on my chest ready to be called upon. There is so much that we do that often goes unnoticed or unappreciated. I think we should lobby to have Mother's Day once a month instead of once a year. That way, we can be recognized for all that we do on a daily basis. Mothers make the world go round.

That said, with great power comes great responsibility. It is the job of a mother to ensure that the household is one filled with love and joy. It can be hard to focus on being all full of love and joy when you just don't feel like it or you are dealing with getting through the day and everyone seems to want to push your "last reserve nerve button." No one said that creating serenity in the midst of chaos would be easy, but the mom who wants to do it, can. We make the decision to want to do it.

There is a book I mentioned earlier, entitled *The Seven Minute Difference: Small Steps to Big Changes* by Allyson Lewis. This is such a tremendous book, and I highly recommend it for anyone who desires to do small things that can have a lifelong effect. I credit this book with forcing me to think about what kind of mother I wanted to be and then giving me the tools by which to do it.

Mrs. Lewis espouses that her book is for the executive or business person who wants to grow, as well as anyone else who wants to tap into their potential. As a stay-at-home-mom and COO of Personnel Development and Operations, I wanted to become the best COO I could be for my household. I learned how doing small things could have an impact on my week and positively affect my entire household and outlook on our future.

I learned that in seven minutes, I can write a sincere note to a friend. I can print out a shopping list of things I normally buy, making food shopping easy and convenient. I can read a book to my children before bedtime. I would have thought that these things would consume so much more time, but Mrs. Lewis' book made me realize that by asking myself tough questions, and putting a time limit on my answer, great things spilled out.

Having to figure out what my true heart's desire was, baffled me and I could not narrow my ideas down. Now I can. My heart's desire is to grow into being the absolute best mom and wife I can be while not forgetting who I am as a woman. I craft my future actions around this desire and everything I do is meant to further each of these life goals.

Being a mother can be a difficult task because kids don't come with instructions. However, our task can be more manageable when we have goals and a clear direction we desire to pursue. At the beginning of the week, take a few minutes and write down one to two things you want to accomplish that week to make your family happy. It can be small or large, just write down one thing that you, as mom, can do that is different.

Make dessert during the week and then allow the kids to sit with you in bed while you read a story. Allow the kids to watch TV one school morning after they have gotten ready and eaten breakfast. Let the kids plan family night and help make dinner. Write notes to different family members letting them know you love them. Take turns taking silly pictures of one another and then make a photo album or book. Whatever it is, do something to build up memories of being a "fun mom" who enjoys her children and isn't afraid to show it.

BRINGING SEXY BACK – MOTHER

I know some reading this believe it's almost oxymoronic to think that a mother can be sexy. Well, momma, it isn't. I remember being pregnant with Victoria and Jimmy. My attire was very demure and low-key. Even in a dream, I wouldn't have put on a bathing suit or considered getting trendy clothing. Not only could we not afford it, I didn't have the time to shop for clothes that I would only wear during pregnancy.

During that time, my mind did not think that motherhood was sexy. It was like oil and water: no matter how much you shake or stir, the two just don't mix. I had a very outdated belief that the motherhood glow was the only beautiful thing about motherhood. Even after Victoria and Jimmy were born, I still did not think that a mother should expose any part of her body, even her knees. To me, it was setting a bad example for my children to see me dress in a v-neck or sleeveless shirt, or wear pants that were form fitting. I didn't see these types of clothing as "motherly." I remember many conversations with my grandmother about how a woman should carry herself and the types of modest clothing she should wear. My grandmother said that by exposing my body, I was sending out the signal that I was "loose" and that no one would take me seriously and see that I was intelligent. That stuck with me throughout my childhood and well into adulthood. I had a matronly attitude that was dated and in desperate need of modernization.

When I found out I was pregnant with Ella, I confessed to James that I was tired of being dowdy and I wanted to be a hot, sexy, pregnant mother. Before my physical appearance could change, I had to make the mental transition from matronly to trendy. For the first time in my entire pregnant life, I purchased cute and stylish maternity clothes. I even bought a maternity swimsuit and unashamedly showed off my big belly at a pool party.

With my previous pregnancies, I wore lots of hand-me-downs and bought larger-sized clothing that I could eventually wear again. I vowed that this would no longer be acceptable. I had been exposed to so many cute pregnant women with great bodies who were healthy, and looked great. I was challenged in my beliefs and acceptance that I could be pregnant and sexy, too.

I achieved my goal of being a sexy pregnant woman not consumed with each lump, bump, or roll. I worked out, drank plenty of water, and loved being me. I "wore" pregnancy; pregnancy didn't "wear" me. My mindset was what really determined how I felt about being comfortable in my own skin. I loved being pregnant, and I loved being a sexy pregnant mother.

As a mother of three, I believe I am sexy. I have an understanding that I always want to look my best. Sometimes my best involves a warm-up suit, sneakers, and baseball cap. Sometimes it involves getting dressed, putting on make-up and doing my hair. Whatever it is, I have to make the effort to be sexy and walk tall.

As stated earlier, I am aware that I am setting the example of whom I want my children to follow. I want my daughters to know that they can be stylish in their choice of clothing and still remain modest. I want my son to know and see that a woman can be "covered up" and be gorgeous and attractive. I don't want any of them to think that there is anything wrong with sexiness as an expression of who they are or what they desire.

I take issue with using sex appeal to cover up inadequacies or low self-esteem. I teach my children that the person they are on the inside is far more important than the outer shell, but in our society, they need to balance that with always presenting themselves positively and to the best of their abilities. Even without saying this they all have fashion sense. Like James, Jimmy can look in a closet and pick out a dashing outfit that accentuates his positives. Victoria has fashion plate written all over her; she has been coordinating fashion-forward styles since she could walk. Even Ella knows which shoes she wants to wear with what outfit and purse. The saddest part is that all my children out-style me, almost on a daily basis.

Victoria and Ella are teaching me how to be a girl and not a tomboy. On one shopping trip, I casually said to Victoria, "You're going to have to teach me how to shop for clothes." Victoria looked at me with a serious face and said, "Mom, I'm so happy you asked me. Let's start with a new belt, shoes and purse!" Accessorizing is what makes an outfit, and if I have to enroll my children in helping me to do it, then, so be it. I am not so grown up that I don't need help, even if it is from a seven-year-old.

James loves me so much and takes pity on me. He knows I hate to shop for clothes, so he knows me and when I need something, he picks it up for me. Ninety-nine percent of the time, he hits the nail on the head. I adore that about him and thank him for rescuing me from having to do it. (I know it's crazy, that I am a mother of two girls and one boy yet I hate to go clothes shopping.)

Part of bringing yourself to a place of being a sexy mother involves discovering your definition of sexy. Get help to focus your thoughts and style to make it a reality. Bring Sexy Back to a place of prominence in your life. If it was never there, start today. If it is slightly lost, turn on the neon flashing sign and say, "I am HERE!"

> *"Dad needs to show an incredible amount of respect and humor and friendship toward his mate so the kids understand their parents are sexy, they're fun, they do things together, they're best friends. Kids learn by example. If I respect Mom, they're going to respect Mom."*
>
> – Tim Allen

NOTES:

CHAPTER 9

DAILY MENTAL HEALTH BREAKS

"By and large, mothers and housewives are the only workers who do not have regular time off. They are the great vacationless class."
— Anne Morrow Lindbergh

By now, you should know or maybe you have discovered that you are phenomenal. Now that you know what to do, learn how to do it. A key part to being sexy is having a positive mental state. I would even venture to say that over 90% of sexiness is mentally related and the other 10% is the physical manifestation of that inner beauty. Learning to set your mind on things that are peaceful and bigger than you are, is where you want to start. I make it a daily practice to take some sort of mental health break for at least 10-30 minutes. If you are a morning person, take it during the early morning hours before anyone wakes up. If you're a night owl like me, stay up a few minutes after everyone is asleep and bask in the serenity of a quiet house. If you run from sunrise to sunset, then maybe you need to carve out a niche of time during the day.

Take time out to recharge your mental batteries so you can continue to function daily. I know of many women who take breaks and those who do not. Some women I know have a desire to be around their children all day and night because it gives them a certain satisfaction. Other women need to be around their children because they find their identity in being needed by their children.

There is absolutely nothing wrong with either of these positions. However, I believe they will eventually need to take time apart from their children for several reasons. First, they need to show their children that they must learn to amuse themselves without needing others to stimulate them. This statement is not for those parents with differently-abled children, only for those whose children are not differently-abled.

Secondly, it teaches the child how to trust others besides you. If children are around only you, it sends a very clear yet subtle message that you do not trust anyone other than you and they shouldn't either. Part of growing up is learning to trust parents as well as others; it is vital to becoming a fully developed adult who makes good decisions and bonds relationally.

THAT IS SELFISH

> "I feel selfish needing a break from my children. It is my responsibility to teach and train my children to the best of my ability. If I say I need a break, I am almost admitting that I am a failure as a parent and that I don't love my children. I should be able to spend all day and night with my children, without a break, to affect them and show them that I love them."

These statements are all fused and steeped in guilt, misperception and untruth. There is absolutely nothing wrong with needing time for yourself. There is nothing selfish about recharging. Think of it in terms of school. Every year, teachers get weeks and even months off from school at certain intervals. Is it because the students just can't absorb any more information? Could it be because students and teachers alike need some time to absorb all that they have learned? Even the most devoted educator, looks forward to the breaks.

Yes, it is the responsibility of the parent to do all that he or she can do to teach the child. However, there has to come a point when both of you need some "quiet time" to absorb all that was learned and to decompress alone.

Just like a bank, if all you do is continually give to others and make withdrawals, eventually you will be bankrupt and have nothing else to give to yourself or anyone else. What good are you to anyone if you never give to yourself or deposit (small or large amount) time to recharge? I have talked with thousands of parents who have expressed a very clear need to ensure they have time by themselves. Some parents have indicated that they need as little as 15 minutes or up to two hours. Whatever time is needed for you, don't feel guilty about taking it.

You are not a failure as a parent if you admit that you need a break. You are admitting that you are human, and human beings require time alone. Babies need quiet time daily to decompress; adults are no different. Embrace your humanity and don't rely on being "SuperMom" all the time.

If we really love our child, we will show them that it is OK to take care of oneself in the daily task of caring for others. I can't state that anymore simply. If we embrace being an example to our children and want them to follow in our footsteps, we will show a positive example of self-love.

Please clear your mind of thinking that taking time for yourself is wrong or wasteful. Embrace needing to show yourself just how great life can be by taking time daily to discover your destiny and explore your thoughts, hobbies, and role as a parent.

There are so many things you can do during your downtime. You are smart and know what you enjoy. Step into the business of discovering your hobbies or even time with your own thoughts. Whatever it is, make it about you, and what you enjoy doing. Even if you enjoy helping others and want to do something for someone else, there is no problem because you are doing something that makes you happy.

MY PARENTS NEVER NEEDED A BREAK

We think that because our parents never needed a break, we don't either. If your parents are around, ask them what kind of break they needed. I guarantee they will say they not only took breaks, but also enjoyed those breaks to the fullest. My mother used to send us to stay with our aunts and uncles in the South during the summer. We would spend at least three to four weeks discovering the countryside and learning how to do new things. Although we were "city kids," we had fun learning how the "country kids" did things. It was such a great time and we enjoyed ourselves. As children, we never categorized this break as "Mommy's time alone." To this day, we don't know what my mother did. All we know is that when we got back, she was happier and more relaxed.

If your parents aren't around, ask someone that you admire or whose parenting skills you respect. Ask them what they do to relax, what time their children go to bed and how they came up with that time? I imagine that you will find they take time every day to do something for themselves. They may send their children to bed early so they can spend time with their spouse or by themselves. In the past 20 years, I have yet to meet a parent who was refreshed and revived, yet spent 100% of their time with their child. If you are that anomaly, please blog about it and tell others and me how you manage to do it. I always like to learn new things and would enjoy reading about it.

When you watch television, you may be led to believe that women on these shows don't need a break, and neither do you. Other than the obvious fact that someone scripts what happens, it is totally wrong. Every television mom somehow needs an outlet. When you look for it in your favorite show (Claire Huxtable from the *Cosby Show* was mine), you will see that she does it by going on dates, being with her friends, volunteering or doing some sort of hobby. Modern day moms also add trips to the spa for manicures and pedicures, or blogging and girl time, or similar activity.

By scheduling time for yourself, you are on your way to creating the atmosphere of being an amazing mom. You are showing your family that you value yourself and them. You create opportunities to both showcase your talents and be an example for your children. Your daily mental health break allows you to reexamine your goals and ensure that the vision you have set is on course. If you have deviated, this is the time where you can get back to where you were initially headed. If you have not had the opportunity to create a vision of where you want to be as a mom, take some time to do it during this break time.

"Don't compromise yourself. You are all you've got."
– Janis Joplin

NOTES:

CHAPTER 10

PHYSICAL EXERCISE-UGH!!

"If it weren't for the fact that the TV set and the refrigerator are so far apart, some of us wouldn't get any exercise at all."

– Joey Adams

For me, physical exercise used to be two of the foulest words in the English language. In the glory days of high school, I used to be able to eat anything I wanted and still remain a size six. Once I hit college, that all changed. For some reason, my metabolism changed and I could no longer eat nonstop and stay thin. I had to work at it. I played volleyball and softball. I would also make sure I worked up a sweat when I went dancing. Once I graduated college I stopped playing sports and had to join a gym to keep my weight under 150 pounds.

After two babies, my weight loss goal became 150 pounds, as I weighed over 180 pounds. I still have yet to reach my goal of 150 pounds, but in the back of my mind, I will do it one day (maybe). Right now, my goal is to look and feel healthy. If healthy is 155 pounds and toned, I am happy with that. My focus is overall general health, not to become super thin.

I used to be concerned with my weight as I stared in the mirror at my muffin top, flab and cottage cheese. I don't know where it all came from and how it snuck up on me (wait, I do know and their names are Victoria, Jimmy, Olivia, and Gabriella). What I do know is that I need to firm it up and stop the wiggle and jiggle. My personal goals inspire me to work hard to achieve them. We can all have the bodies we desire if we start with a hefty dose of determination coupled with physical exercise, and rounded off with a healthy eating plan.

DIETING YO-YO

As part of my "sexy mama" phase, I decided I wanted to lose about 25 pounds. Initially, I joined a gym. I started cardio-kickboxing classes and had a free consultation with a personal trainer. I asked him to design a plan that I could do on my own. Through this method, I lost nearly 18 pounds and about nine inches over my body. I was pleased and felt better about myself.

The greatest thing about the gym was that they offered childcare as part of the membership. I could go for two hours daily and work out while my children played and were supervised by someone other than me. James says he loved that I was going to the gym because I was happier and less stressed. I agreed that this was a pleasant side effect. I took time out for me, and exercised at the same time. There were a few days where I didn't exercise at all, but instead, I sat in the café drinking a latte and reading a book, all because I could!

Unfortunately, I stopped going because they changed the times of my favorite classes and stopped offering one of them all together. At times, I reminisce and think I should join a gym again. Is it worth the monthly fee to be stress-free? I would love to say yes, yes, YES! However, you have to decide for yourself and see if it can work within your budget and schedule.

A year after I stopped going to the gym, I decided I needed to get back on the weight loss side of things and stabilize my eating as I had regained more than 20 pounds. I owned over 15 different workout tapes at home; I just wasn't motivated to do any of them. I decided to kickstart things by joining two healthy-living websites (www.ediets.com then www.sparkpeople.com). I started the plan and site weighing 179 pounds.

Within five months, I had lost 20 pounds and was down to 159 pounds. I enjoyed doing exercise challenges, talking with others about my goals, my shortfalls, stumbles, and triumphs. It was so much fun and I became great friends with my weight-loss pals. After nearly four years, we are all still in contact with one another, even though we are no longer on the weight-loss site. We shared so much about our lives that we became invested in one another. Although I have never met any of my weight-loss pals in person, some of them have met and had fun weekends together. Ange, Yanya, Jennibean, and Belle are amazing people who have been a pillar of strength and wealth of knowledge on my journey.

I learned that the most important thing about healthy-living is the idea getting drilled into my head to stop short-term dieting. "Diet" is a lifestyle change and refers to how one eats and lives. Yes, I will go through phases where I may need to shed some unwanted pounds, but if I focus on eating right and exercising, that process is easy, not arduous. The sites also taught me the difference between "eating to live" versus "living to eat." The former promotes health while the later promotes unhealthy eating habits (emotional or unconscious eating). I learned that dieting and physical exercise are a lifestyle choice.

Initially, the program seemed daunting. I wondered if I would have time to exercise regularly. If I ran out of things to do, would I get sick and tired of doing the same exercises? Worst yet, what would I do when I reached my goal and lost those despised 25 pounds? Would I stop exercising and coast? What would happen if I stopped and then started gaining weight back again, only to have to work harder to lose it all again?

I kept thinking to myself that it wasn't worth the hassle. I could live with being a size 14 and eventually buy bigger clothing. The main thing that stopped me from talking myself out of my goal was being winded while playing in the yard with the kids. How in the world could a young 30-year-old get winded playing in the yard with a couple of toddlers? This was unreal to me.

I didn't know how I allowed myself to gain such unhealthy weight. I had the audacity to yell at James. I asked him, "Why didn't you say something to me when you saw me getting larger and larger by the day?"

His response made me cross my eyes in frustration, "Honey, you look at yourself in the mirror every day. Don't you know what you look like? You know I love you no matter what."

I wanted to strangle him. That was the worst non-answer in the world. He was right though, and it forced me to examine my problem areas and figure out how best to attack them so they would tighten up.

I had so many questions that didn't seem to have an answer until I got on the site and began to follow the plan. I found out that if I built in "crash days," I would be able to eat some sweets and all those not-so-good foods and still be able to maintain my weight-loss and lifestyle goals.

I also learned that exercise was a relative term. On my non-weight or cardio-focused days, I could merely do something that promoted my overall general health. I could take a walk, take the stairs in a building, park at the far end of the parking lot and walk to the store, or use my groceries as weights.

I learned so much and was continually encouraged from the site, but more from the people on the site who had either achieved their goals, were in the midst of achieving their goals, or those who were new and forced me to remember the basics. I found out that some of my workout tapes could be used for many of the message board challenges. I also invested in a couple of new workout programs that I still use. I had to be real with myself and make those hundreds of invested dollars in workout DVDs pay off in usage. If you're curious about a workout tape, check it out at the public library or rent it at the video store first.

BENEFITS

We all know that there are a number of benefits to exercising. First though, we have to convince ourselves of those benefits and mentally cross-reference it with our life goals, thus creating a formula for success. I had to have the life experience of getting winded while playing with my children to help me understand that my health condition did not promote being able to play with my children. If I continued to gain weight, I might suffer other health problems that would stop me from seeing my children grow up.

This information smacked me in the face, and I came to the realization that if I wanted to become the best mom in the world, I had to be around. I became invested in seeing my children and grandchildren grow up. I made a conscious effort to monitor my food consumption and exercise. I didn't deny myself some guilty pleasures on occasion, but I also made the choice to not devour them at record pace either. It was a daily chore for me, but I had to practice restraint and start making good choices to conquer my temptations. I still struggle with this, but I can say I have more good days than bad. Get to the place where you start making more good choices, and you will begin seeing the benefits of those choices.

How will becoming physically active benefit your life? Are you already doing something to maintain your overall health? If so, how can you take it up a notch to ensure that you not only maintain your health but become an inspiration to someone else? We are helpers one to another. If we have achieved a level of success, how can we help someone else reach their goals and support them on their journey?

If you're physically active, you're more likely to have less tension and a regulated mood. You feel better regardless of the environment you're in and have fewer negative thoughts. You may be more willing to help those around you because of an increased energy level.

Living a sedentary life will more than likely be the opposite of all that is listed above. If you allow those endorphins to be released in your body, you will have created a natural mood regulator and done something for yourself and those you love.

The biggest benefit of all....skinny jeans! Hello! Seriously though, it is great being able to wear the clothes in your closet or buying new ones. Whether you're one of the rare women who are working hard to gain weight, or you are currently wearing plus sizes, we all want to be fit and feel good about ourselves. When you can become physically active and fit at any size and age, that is the reward, not the jeans.

PREGNANCY AND EXERCISE

Earlier in the book, I talked about how I got pregnant and then miscarried with Olivia. I thought my exertion level at the gym was one of the factors. However, the best outcome for my physical exercise was Gabriella. She became an ever-present reminder of my redemptive exercise program. In the eight months between my miscarriage of Olivia and conception of Gabriella, I went on an all-out attack on stress and weight gain. I started working out at home with my tapes and using what I learned on the message boards. Once I finally got my weight down to 156 pounds, I not only looked and felt great, I fit into my clothes in a way I had not done in years. My confidence level exuded out of every pore in my body.

It was not until the sight of chicken made me ill that I took the pregnancy test and realized that God had blessed me with a baby. I was excited, but at the same time, God's sense of humor and timing plagued me. Why would He, in His infinite wisdom, grant me my petition of having a baby only after I had lost over 23 pounds and looked and felt better than I had in years? I really wanted to know. It was not until I stopped and realized that I was in peak physical and mental condition that I saw the wisdom unveiled.

While pregnant, I drank 80+ ounces of water daily along with taking multivitamins and eating healthy. I employed the principles of proper food combining to make sure not to go backwards in my battle of weight. I ate what I needed and did not reduce my food intake. Because of this, my body gained "good" weight that sustained and supported my eight-pound, six-ounce baby girl. I gained a total of 23 pounds, and once Ella was born, I lost all the weight within a matter of two weeks. I looked as though I had never been pregnant, yet I hadn't worked out in the traditional sense. During pregnancy, I walked around the grocery store and did very low-impact strength exercises for 20 minutes, three times per week.

Post-pregnancy, I was able to maintain my pre-pregnancy weight of 156 pounds for nearly eight months after delivering Ella. However, my post-pregnancy downfall came in not getting back to my full exercise program immediately. I completely relapsed and strayed from all that I had learned. I had exercise amnesia. I rationalized it as being busy with the three children and not having time to fit exercise into my day. I knew this was not true and I should have found the time by rescheduling other activities. The end is that I gained back about nine pounds of bad weight and weighed 165 pounds. It was not until I got serious about my health that I started to combat that weight. I am now on the downward slope of getting back to a healthy range (for my height, frame, and age) of less than 160 pounds.

The moral of this story is that being physically active helps you to weather pregnancy, post-pregnancy, and a busy life. If you choose to remain sedentary, the weight will stay and then accumulate causing a very vicious cycle. Make it your desire to do something, even if it is not formalized or organized. Getting a companion or buddy to be your support always helps motivate and keep you accountable. Start small and then build up endurance as well as length. If you can get started with 15 minutes of heart-pumping activity per day, you are on your way to creating a happier and healthier you.

My husband and I are currently working out together, and we keep each other accountable to our goals and push one another to go past our perceived personal limits (codeword for excuses). Initially, find someone, to stay motivated and accountable to, and remember how good it feels to work out. It may be hard to start, but once you do, it feels great. It's all about the endorphins, baby!

> *"I don't exercise. If God had wanted me to bend over, he would have put diamonds on the floor."*
> – Joan Rivers

NOTES:

CHAPTER 11

RELATIONSHIPS

"You never lose by loving. You always lose by holding back."

– Barbara DeAngelis

SPOUSAL

My spousal relationship is one that I depend upon heavily. My husband is my best friend and helper. He helps me stay balanced and I depend on him for emotional stability. He helps make the load of caring for the home more manageable.

We decided early on that as a dedicated father, James would actively participate in the lives of the children on a daily basis. Along with eating dinner as a family, he decided to take on the responsibility of the evening ritual (bathing, dressing, reading a story, and praying with the kids). This gives him the opportunity to spend quality time with the children and hear about their days while investing time in them. By doing this, he gives me the opportunity to decompress before we spend time with each other.

I love that my husband is able to do this for our family. His investment into our family is tremendous and will reap a great reward in the future. Not only does he have a strenuous day at work, he then comes home and helps with the kids. On the weekends, he and my mother give me a break from the weekly chores by cooking. I am truly grateful to him for all that he does and how amazing of a father he is to the children.

A spousal relationship can help you grow and mature as a person because it forces you to get outside of yourself and deal with another person who is in your space. You know, the same someone who leaves the toothpaste cap off of the toothpaste, or pushes it up from the top, or eats the last piece of cake that you have been craving all day long. What about if you're a quiet person and your spouse is someone who needs music, television, and appliances on all at the same time?

You have the makings of a very cramped household (personality wise). By marrying, you decide to grow and not stay in your own shell expecting everyone to adjust to you. In our case, that process took James and me about a year. Once we adjusted, we learned to accept each other's weaknesses. However, the areas of strength that once attracted us to each other, we now bumped heads over. It's amazing that the once highly thought of qualities became a thorn in our sides. You know qualities like determination and being strong-willed. After years of marriage, we have come to embrace and love each other's weaknesses and strengths. James is the Yang to my Yin! I love him more today than when we first got married. It is not easy, and we do have some rough spots; we have simply chosen to love each other through the storms rather than allow the storms to dictate who we are and how our relationship is defined.

The spousal relationship has to be nurtured, and just as your spouse helps you, you have to pour into your spouse and help him. Your spouse is not only there to assist you, (even though he is your help mate). He is there to be helped by you too! Start to love on your spouse the minute he walks through the door. Say a kind word as you give him a hug and kiss. During dinner, make it a point to draw him into the conversation or allow him to lead the dinner discussion. Make sure to put the kids in bed early enough that you have time to dedicate to your spouse.

Originally, we put the kids in the bed sometime around 8:30pm or 9pm, but eventually decided they needed more sleep and we needed more time. We finally started putting them to bed around 7:30pm. That extra hour made it much easier for us to transition from putting the kids down to having time for us. It gave us freedom that we had not known previously. We had our own personal time back. It is to the point now, that if the kids are up past 8pm, we get antsy and start shooing them off (minus weekends) because our time is being delayed. I understand that this time adjustment may not fit your family. Don't get hung up on the 7:30pm bedtime. Get focused on the "idea" of making time daily to spend with your spouse.

We have also made it a priority to plan weekly family nights and have quarterly dating with our children. Family nights are scheduled for Friday nights. Sometimes we watch movies, go bowling, play video games, go out for ice cream, spend hours in the park, play board games, or hold camp-ins in the living room. The kids look forward to it and depend on it happening.

We recently began teaching our children the fundamentals of dating. We do the whole thing, from getting dressed up to going out to having the men pay for dinner. Before the date, James and I talk to our same-gender children and coach them on our standards for proper "date etiquette." James gives Jimmy money so that he can get in the habit of paying for dinner and makes him do extra chores during the week so that he can earn extra money for his date with Mom. It's really sweet, because he wants to be like his dad and provide a great date for me because he has "The best mom in the whole wide world!"

With Victoria, I talk with her about how to let her dad be a gentleman and open doors, pull out chairs, pay for dinner and hold her hand. She is my quintessential girl, so she expects it. I love it because as I watch her grow and mature, she is so feminine and dainty that I constantly learn from her. To balance her personality with my practicality, I give her money to put in her purse (just in case), along with the explanation that if something goes wrong, she can pay for the meal and tip. Like Jimmy, she too, has to do extra chores to get additional money for her dates. On her first date with Dad, she was adamant that she wanted to pay for dinner because she had the money. Dad had to talk her down off the ledge, smiling the whole time. I guess he saw me in her because I used to do that to him when we went out. I have since learned to let him do what makes him happy.

Dating our children has given us the opportunity to affect our children's expectations of dates. It has also allowed us to set the foundation of respect, trust, and chivalry. By "dating" them now, when the time comes for them to do it later in life, we know what will happen, and the standard that has been set.

SINGLES

If you are leading a single-parent household, here are a few things you may be able to do to find sanity and still be able to give back.

Being a single-parent can be made more manageable by doing some of the following: registering for a Big Brother/Big Sister mentor program, finding a friend who can take your children for one day a week while you get some personal time, arranging for a family member to help you raise the children, or maintaining a cordial relationship with the other parent of the children. If you have an opposite-gender child, it is important to find a positive same-gender role model for that child. Your child will be able to relate and receive guidance from a different perspective.

I remember growing up with no father figure and my mother worked hard to support us. I had two special teachers who picked up much of the slack and were able to deposit positive things in my life. I had a male eighth-grade science teacher named, Mr. Bacetti, and female English teacher named, Mrs. Russell, who took a keen interest in me and my group of friends. We were mostly from single-parent households, and they knew it. Both teachers became friends and mentors. As they taught us to excel in our studies, we learned valuable life skills. Mr. Bacetti taught the young men how to be young men, while Mrs. Russell taught us how to carry ourselves as young ladies with high standards.

If the male parent is around, please let him be involved in the life of his child (barring any type of abuse). Part of maintaining a cordial relationship with the child's other parent serves as maturity among the parents and continues to reaffirm your child with love. The parents, not the child caused the separation. To make the child suffer, or worst yet, to use the child as a pawn is selfish, and possibly hurtful in the long-run to your relationship with the child.

When I was six-years-old, my parents separated. I became slightly resentful towards my mother. I respected her, but from my perspective as a six-year-old child, I just didn't comprehend. Despite my Dad's alcoholism and abuse, I was a forgiving child who still wanted and needed her dad. At times, I felt like I was in a tug of war between my parents, and it wasn't fair to me. I followed instructions because I wanted to be an obedient daughter who loved my mother and did all that she asked, without question. However, my dad would often present ideas that made it appear as though he wanted me in his life while my mother wanted to keep me from him. The result was that I unintentionally harbored resentful feelings towards my mother which built up and festered through to adulthood.

While I was in college, my dad was on his deathbed, and a wave of feelings and emotions came flooding out of me. On one occasion, my father asked my mother to come to the hospital so he could apologize to her for all he had done wrong. It took every ounce of courage and pleading I could muster to make this happen. Because of the intense love of my mother for me, she came. For a brief time in their presence, I was that six-year-old girl who felt the love of both mother and father. After it was all done, I saw how draining it had been to my mother and finally understood how deeply she had been hurt. It was on that day I understood that my mother would do anything to make the hurt of her child stop. I gained a newfound knowledge of seeing things through a mother's eyes that had never been present before.

As a product of a separated household (due to physical and mental abuse), I know it can be difficult to maintain a relationship with someone whom you are severely angry, and who has hurt you tremendously. When you keep the child at the forefront of your minds, it will keep your perspective directed toward the child.

You have to act in the best interests of the child. Eventually, you may be able to find something to communicate about, even if it is allowing that parent to speak on the phone to the child to say, "I love you." Remember, we are models for the behavior we want our children to exhibit when they are older. Work hard towards modeling the behavior you would love to see happen. Like I said, I understand that this is a challenging area and may need to be developed as a process over time. It may even be necessary to cut off all communication for safety's sake. You have to do what you deem necessary for your child's safety and well-being.

Finding a mentor program can help your child have an outlet to do fun things that only someone of the same gender can relate to. It gives the child more than an hour of time where they can be entertained by another's company. The child may ask questions and receive good instruction. Mentor programs have such a diverse appeal and there are so many benefits to all parties involved. Search your local community, religious organization, and personal network to see what resources are available.

UNINVOLVED PARTNERS

If you have a spouse who is uninvolved, it can be very frustrating and make you feel as though you are single. The question is how to get your spouse involved so that you are NOT overwhelmed, nor is your family missing out on the benefits of two active parents.

One of the first steps is to have an open discussion of expectations on what each of you is prepared to do to fix the disparity. As a reality check for you, once you ask for help, DON'T criticize your spouse. Also, DON'T say you could have done it better. Accept the level of help that is being offered and allow it to grow and get better over time.

If your spouse is wholly unwilling to talk and help, there is more at stake. You may have to be more patient and allow that spouse room to grow into what you need him to be by giving suggestions and overt pointers. Ultimately, you will have to figure out a way to draw your spouse into your world so you can effectively help everyone else. If professional counseling is an option, propose the idea and see how he feels about it.

DON'T have false or extremely robust expectations of your spouse. Whether you are a working mother or stay-at-home-mom, the family responsibilities should be shared. The best times to discuss these are while dating. I say dating because you get an opportunity to understand each other's personalities and determine what you expect of the other person. If your spouse is uninvolved, it is self-defeating to believe he will automatically do a complete 180-degree turn once you are married with children and become completely involved. Involvement is a process that takes time to build. To minimize frustration, have realistic expectations and proceed with baby steps of inclusion.

Those expectations will often evolve as life's situations change. It may be that you have to bear the brunt of the responsibility, and at others, your spouse will have to step in and do most of the work. Whatever it is, make sure that constant nagging is not a part of how you communicate. Nothing will make a person tune out faster than continual discussion about how they are not living up to expectations. You may not be saying these exact words, but if your sentiment is translating this, expect to run up against a brick wall; be prepared to see no further growth or help.

If your spouse is minimally involved due to specific work or school issues (i.e. medical residency or dissertation) communicate the time expectations. It may be a lonely few years, but when he is home, enjoy and maximize the time you have together. Like my friend Tammy says, "She can do anything if she knows it has a purpose and an end time."

PARENTS

Parents and mentors possess a specialized brand of knowledge and can be a wonderful outlet for discussion or comfort. When my mother Myra moved in with our family over three years ago, she helped me more than words could say. As a stay-at-home-mom, I often times needed a break. Having my mother here to watch the kids while I went to an appointment or did chores, made life more manageable.

The kids really appreciate the time spent with their Nana. There is a special bond that is shared and they experience Nana's special brand of love. I remember growing up and spending time with my grandmother. She was tough as nails, not shy, and she would share her opinions with you whether you wanted her to or not. She took to heart the Biblical statements: "Train up a child in the way he should go; and when he is old, he will not depart from it."[8] "Foolishness is bound in the heart of a child; but the rod of correction shall drive it far from him."[9]

I look back on the time we lived with her, and I have loving memories and firm lessons learned. It was an interesting time that helped to mold me into the person I am today. Through being sent back to the store for correct change, I learned the value in counting all money received back from the cashier. When we went shopping, she showed me how to choose the freshest food and where to locate food with the longest expiration dates (most times, look towards the back). Grandma Liz also enforced a very strict standard of obedience. If she said to come into the house at a certain time, I had better be there five minutes early! The most valuable lesson learned was that of hard work; doing it right the first time is better than having to re-do it completely.

A grandmother is a jewel. As a warning, she is not the same person who raised you as a child. Grandmothers take on a whole new personality that is unbelievable. They give kids cookies and sweets every night, freely give away candy, and get kids ice cream when they go out. Grandmothers go to the toy store often, and are now OK with the wild indiscretions of young children.

I was shocked that my mother and my in-laws have become such pushovers. James and I wished they were this way when we were growing up. James often asks his parents, "Where were *you* when we were growing up? I wish you had been this lenient back then. My childhood would have been so easy." In reality, if James and my parents had been lenient while we were growing up, we would be very different people who wouldn't have accomplished many of the things we have done up to this point. The reward for being a great parent is that you can be the best grand and great-grand parent in the world.

In talks with my father-in-law, I discovered that he had a set goal of how he wanted to raise his children and where he wanted them to end up in life. My in-laws were onto something as they raised three successful children: a doctor & Ivy-League graduate, a lawyer and Ivy-League graduate, and a financial services executive and West Point graduate.

My mother single-handedly raised five children: a chef, a communications liaison, a real estate maintenance manager, a former real estate agent, investor & Ivy-League graduate, and a customer service technician. The most successful parents seem to be those who have thought about and actively prepared for the visions they have for their children.

A key factor in that success is ensuring that you build a positive and lasting relationship with your parents. It may be easy for some, and difficult for others. Whatever the circumstances that have led to the relationship you have with your parents, realize that you are setting the example for the type of relationship your children will have with you.

If circumstances prevent you from having a relationship with your natural parents, aim to find an older person with whom you can connect and act as a proxy grandparent to your children. It is important for your children to see your interaction with the more mature segment of the population. This teaches children to respect their elders and learn how they should interact with them. Something gets lost if that relationship is not there. If that relationship is there, it is invaluable and really goes a long way to building a well-rounded individual.

FRIENDS

Do you have a friend? I don't mean an acquaintance or someone whom you know and spend time with. I mean someone whom you trust and respect. Do you have someone in your life that builds you up but is not afraid to tell you when you're wrong? Do you have a woman who is a confidant who you can share your emotions and heart's desire with? If you do not have that person in your life, you need to work on cultivating an existing relationship that can grow into just that.

For years, I had trouble connecting with women, and my best friends were men. There's nothing wrong with having male friendships except there is just something very special about a woman-to-woman bond. I discovered that there are women who, despite my previous experience, wanted the best for me.

During my adolescence, many young women hurt me with betrayal, making it difficult for me to trust women. In college I finally learned to let my guard down. I had to understand sisterhood and was thankful to be accepted into the Rho Chapter of Delta Sigma Theta Sorority, Incorporated. I went through an experience that forced me to bond with a group of young ladies whom I initially did not know very well. By the end of our membership training process, we bonded and learned to trust one another implicitly. It was such an amazing experience and after more than 15 years, we are all still friends, involved at some level in one another's lives.

I have also learned to have well-rounded relationships with other women by joining mom's playgroups and women's groups at different churches. It took some time, but I discovered a kinship with women. When I see one woman hurt, I hurt. When I look at moms smiling at their children, my heart is filled with warmth and I can't help but to smile. There is a freedom that comes from building strong relationships with other women. Even if it is only one or two, make the effort to do it, and you will be rewarded exponentially.

A sister-friend loves at all times and knows when you are in need. She is ready and prepared to offer her help and to love you and your children. She accepts you for who you are but helps you to become better. You may have an occasional disagreement or two, but the mature woman rectifies the situation and heals the breach. A relationship worth keeping is one worth working for and can grow.

The friend I am talking about could be a family member, a childhood friend, someone whom you just met, but have a kinship with, or someone whom you admire but have not yet spent much time. Building the relationship that you can give into and gives back on a continual basis takes time, patience, and love.

CHILDREN

Building a strong relationship with your child is important. In the early years, the relationship primarily focuses on leading, teaching, guiding, influencing, and nurturing. In the middle and teen years, a shift happens and less instruction may be needed, as you become their guide, mentor, and coach. In the adult years, your role may evolve to friend and fountain of wisdom. You will always be your child's parent, but understand that, each stage requires a unique skill set and focus.

When I was a child, my main influencers were my mother and grandmother. In my middle and teen years, my main influencers were my mother, several teachers, and friends (notice the order here). In my adult years, my main influencers are God, my family, and my friends.

Both my mother, Myra, and my grandmother, Liz, chose to make me their pet project when I was young. One disapproving look from either of them made me stop and reevaluate my actions or thoughts. Often, I was allowed to accompany them while they were out. I felt very privileged to learn life's lessons from these two matriarchs.

During my teenage years, I had several teachers guide me in both my studies and personal life. Mrs. Russell taught me to have standards for myself, as a young lady. Mr. Bacetti taught me to demand that young men behave as young men. Mrs. Crowley taught me that the world was my oyster, and I was the only one who could hold me back, academically.

As a teen, I elevated my mother to the level of best friend. We often stayed up late talking about everything. Unfortunately, I violated her trust when I placed, what was an important friendship to me, over the values I had been taught. I think I lost a little bit of her after that point, but I tried desperately to gain it back. As a daughter, I have always needed to be highly thought of by my mother. It took us about a year, but we finally renewed our relationship.

During my college years, I was guided by the moral compass that was instilled in me throughout my childhood. Despite my upbringing, there were times I deviated off the path in pursuit of friendships that were not necessarily beneficial. However, after hearing many church sermons, I was finally ready to listen. I chose to call myself a Christian by attending church regularly and learning more about what and who the Bible said God was. The greater my understanding, the more my life began to reflect my beliefs. God became the primary influencer in my adult life. I now, conduct myself by my beliefs, and every relationship is somehow an example of those beliefs.

Before submitting to the will of God, my mother was still my moral compass. I depended on her so heavily, that my heart was broken after an incident where I felt her actions isolated and abandoned me. This time, the breach caused a 10-year lapse in our familial intimacy. It was only when I fully embraced maturity, my pain, and her actions that I grew up to see beyond the eyes of a daughter. My spiritual relationship guided me to a place of love and forgiveness. I accepted that there were things I did't know and couldn't grasp. I realized that it was not all about me and my feelings. Although I had previously felt wronged, *I apologized* for harboring anger and resentment. I released my mother and myself from the burden that stopped us from loving each other implicitly. It was during this time, I completed my journey towards becoming a "woman." I no longer had childish selfish motives. I learned to focus on others and see things from different perspectives.

It was not an easy journey, but it had to happen. I had to realize that even though I hurt, I was modeling an unacceptable relationship for my daughters. I constantly thought, "Would I want Victoria or Gabriella to react to me that way or feel that way about me?" I put on my big-girl panties and realized my part in the rift. I owned up to it and then apologized. My mother and I may not always be on the same page, but more often than not, we endeavor to love and respect each other in spite of all that has happened. We have a mindset that says we love each other because she is my mother, I am her daughter, and we are friends.

My relationship with Grandma Liz solidified my early relationship with my mother. My grandmother reinforced very valuable character traits in me that taught me to respect my mother for being a single parent who worked hard at being a mother and provider. It was no doubt challenging for Mom to work and take care of five children. Each child was given responsibilities because Mom expected much of us. When we grumbled, she told us, "Even if you don't like this or that, or even me, you WILL respect me!" We learned that our feelings about circumstances would change, but our respect for her was a constant that did not change.

If early in life, my mother had primarily aimed to be my friend before being my parent; my personality was such that I would have been very self-absorbed and deceptive. I would have done any and everything I wanted and not cared about my effect on others. Even though she allowed us to make our own mistakes, she and my grandmother impressed upon us the need to have a high moral and ethical compass. I learned the importance of compassion and diligence. I teach these character traits to my children.

Understanding that our relationship with our children comes from a set of deliberate actions that lay the groundwork for the future, is pivotal. We need to have a parenting plan. This plan is most effective when the children are young, but it can be created regardless of their age. We have to choose to make it happen.

I equate a parenting plan to having a financial plan. If, during the teenage years, you begin saving a small amount every month, by the time you retire, you will have saved and earned a few million dollars. However, if you start saving for retirement when you are in your 40's, you will have to invest more money to be able to sustain yourself. The whole point with saving for retirement is to start saving.

The same can be said for a relationship with your children. If you have built a rock solid relationship with them during their childhood and now have a phenomenal bond, you have invested wisely. If that bond got fractured or you are in need of repairing a breach in the relationship, it can still be done; it just takes more of an investment. My mother and I have chosen to have non-emotional conversations about real issues. During our discussions, we choose to acknowledge the past while not living in the past. We make an earnest effort to deposit new memories on our road to becoming friends. It's not easy, but it does require someone take the first step and make a valiant attempt.

We used to say we'd "try" to make something work or "try to give it our best effort." Every time we tried, we failed. Don't "try" to have a successful relationship. "Trying" is code word for laziness and leads to excuses for why you cannot do what you anticipate. Taking "try" out of your vocabulary and replacing it with "do," will take you one step closer to achieving success in all that you desire to accomplish.

SPIRITUAL

As an adult, I believe it is important to have a spiritual relationship with God, the Father. I grew up in a household where we went to church every Sunday while Grandma Liz was alive. After Grandma Liz's "home-going" service, Mom moved us to a new area and we didn't go to church as often. We became Palm Sunday, Easter, and Mother's Day churchgoers. We were all baptized in our adolescence and attended many a summer vacation Bible school programs. However, I had no concrete understanding of anything associated with church. I went because we were told we had to go.

After moving to our new area, finding a church was not a requirement, nor was our attendance, (except for those holidays

Laundry Can Wait

mentioned above). We were not rooted in the whole religious experience. When I became a teenager, I was disillusioned with church. The same people who talked about singing in the choir or attending church on Sunday, were the same people partying in the clubs and drinking on Friday and Saturday. I didn't think much of church or people who attended because I knew the church was full of hypocrites and I didn't want any part of it. During vacation Bible school lessons, I was taught to associate people's behavior with their faith and belief levels. In turn, my faith in people, especially those who called themselves "Christians" was severely handicapped.

It was not until I went to college that a friend invited me to go with her to church. I heard the message, "You don't know anything." It was about how people presume to know the plan of God or assume there is no God. All we know or think we know is little in comparison with the reality of who God really is and that He created everything and everyone.

Because I attended an Ivy-League institution, I thought I had attained a certain level of knowledge and was "smart." When I heard this preacher telling me I didn't know anything, I got a little indignant and pride puffed me up a little. That man didn't know anything about me, nor did he know what I had been through. I had just enough Biblical knowledge to be dangerous, and that knowledge kept me away from the hypocrites in the church. For all I knew, that preacher was one of the people I needed to avoid, or so I thought. I kept thinking, "He should be telling Sister Susie over there to stop smoking and drinking and shaking her body in the club!"

Despite my internal conversations, my mind heard the message spoken, but I was not ready to accept any of it. I only acquiesced that God knew more than me. This was the first time that I had been confronted, as an adult, by the Word of God. It caused me to think heavily about my own beliefs and shortcomings and I was humbled more at that service than ever before in my life.

Honestly, I was humbled, but not converted in my ways. I still led a less than "holy" life. My picture was probably next to the definition of "sinner" in the dictionary. Every weekend I drank at the clubs and swore worst than a sailor, besides other unmentionable things. About four years after attending this small church, I met a young man by the name of James M. Cadet. He was a very handsome well-dressed US Army officer living in Killeen, TX. It was *just my luck* that the previous year, he had committed his life to Jesus Christ (January 5, 1997). He was what I called a "Bible-thumping-holy-roller." You know, the person who has to mention Jesus or something about church every other sentence in a conversation. Nonetheless, he and I became friends. Although we didn't know it at the time, the hand of God was on our lives and destined us to befriend each other and build a life together.

One night over the phone, he asked me a very important question. His question to me was simple and direct, "Dee, you have so much going on in your life right now and it seems like you are searching for something greater. Would you like to receive Jesus as your personal Lord and Savior?" It came somewhere between the tears and woes of my life. Mentally, I was replaying the scenes from the previous year of feeling alone, incomplete, and sad about my life. I went through a devastating breakup followed by a casual fling or two. I had made the conscious choice to be alone to find out who I was and what I wanted from a relationship. I came to the conclusion that I did not need a man to give my life value, meaning or to complete me. I discovered that choosing to be alone was therapeutic and restorative. Despite all the newfound growth, I still had bouts of loneliness and needed something greater.

Bringing my mind back to James' question, I was surprised, yet something within me said, "Why not? What do I have to lose?" I knew what he was asking me. I was searching for something, but I was not sure if I wanted to give up all the sinfully fun things I enjoyed doing.

After my internal struggle and a long awkward silence, I decided to say this simple prayer: *"Lord, forgive me of my sins. I ask you to come into my life as my Lord and Savior. Amen."* On April 15, 1998, I became a professed Christian. The skies didn't open, nor did angels appear in my bedroom. However, I did have an immediate peace about the situations I had been experiencing. I thanked James, and after we talked more, I got off the phone. When I awoke the next morning, I made the choice to do my best to follow the prayer I had said the night before.

Even though I had finally received Jesus into my heart, I still didn't give up my sinful ways. I minimized the amount of profanity I used, but I still struggled in all the other areas. I felt bad, but I did not feel like I needed to fully convert and "do right."

A few months later, I started regularly attending a church. I learned that the Holy Spirit was my Helper and Comforter. I read that He would pray for me when I either couldn't or didn't know what to pray for. He would also give me answers to my questions. As a new believer, I wanted to test out what I had been taught. There were many days where I read the Bible and prayed for the Holy Spirit to help me understand and apply what I was reading. I started in Psalms and then made my way to the New Testament. The more I read, the more it seemed like God was showing me areas that I had always wondered about and questioned.

God showed me that my questionable behavior was a mask for hurts from my past. By reading the Bible, going to church, and learning how to pray, I was enlightened as to how certain behaviors were damaging to me as a woman. I discovered how to be whole and complete in Jesus and allow Him to satisfy me. I no longer looked to men to give me all I needed to fill my emotional love tank. For the first time in my adult life, I truly felt free, and it was exhilarating.

One and a half years after meeting James, I moved to Texas. We attended a dynamic ministry named, New Zion Christian Fellowship. I learned more in six months there than I had in my entire life. The word of God had strengthened me and made me a new person. I gained insight and became firmly rooted in my belief. Some of my New York friends thought I was crazy because of how avidly outspoken against church I had been previously.

By choosing to partner up with Jesus, I became a better person. I relied on Him so much when James and I went through rough patches. I prayed to Jesus every time our job or financial situation became unpredictable. I learned to speak the word of God every time one of the children got sick or went through a troublesome time in their life. When I had the miscarriage of Olivia, I was devastated and turned to Jesus as my Healer and Deliverer. He healed me in ways no person ever could. I learned to rejoice no matter the situation or season. I was resolute in my knowledge. I knew that my faith would carry me through anything as long as I kept Jesus as the focus in my life.

The most important spiritual lesson I learned was that I needed to have a solid relationship with God. People may disappoint me, but God the Father is the only one who never disappoints me. Life may throw me some tough and horrendous situations, I may make poor choices, but God will use all the negative things that happen to me, for my good. He does not cause bad things to happen, but He will help and guide me through them all. My relationship with God boils down to how much I trust Him and allow Him to guide me. He wants me to CHOOSE to allow Him to lead me. The more I learn of Him, the more I trust Him and the greater our relationship. Initially, it was difficult and took lots of time and patience. However, the thought of allowing the Supernatural Creator of the Universe to step into my situations far outweighed my doubts.

I hope that reading my testimony helps you to know that Jesus cares and loves you no matter who you are. He wants to be there for you regardless of the situation. He has nothing but good thoughts for you. Even if you don't believe He is real, I testify to you otherwise. Don't let what you think you know, or even what you don't know of Jesus, keep you from getting to know Him more intimately. He wants a relationship with you and has nothing but the best intentions.

He is a gentleman who simply asks that you accept Him into your life. He will never abandon you. He will stick with you through any situation. Jesus will rejoice in every victory and love you through every challenge. Our misconception of love often keeps us from understanding the fullness and depth of his acceptance and availability. Unlike most of us, He doesn't hold a grudge and forgives easily. He wants your heart and faith. He can work with anything small to build it up and make it mighty.

If you have never prayed, or even if you have, but need a refresher, I invite you to say this quick prayer out loud.

"Jesus, please forgive me for all my sins. I ask right now that you come into my life and be my Lord and Savior. Amen."

It's that simple and easy. God is faithful and will honor your prayer. Life may not have gotten 100% better by tomorrow morning, but know that you have just invited a supernatural, heavenly being into your human situation. He is that big and He is that able.

Why is all of this important? As a woman, I rely on my spiritual relationship to maintain sanity and love for others. I have compassion for others because Jesus first had compassion for me. As a wife, I need my spiritual relationship because Jesus has modeled the marriage relationship with the church, and it is a model for my relationship with my husband. As a mother, I need my spiritual relationship so that I can teach and train my children as Christ teaches me. I have to train my children in the way they should go, so that they will learn to love, respect and choose Jesus for themselves.

On the other side of the coin, if you are one of the many who have been hurt by church members or family members who professed Christ, I am truly sorry for that. We are all capable of hurting others and making mistakes; it is only when we learn to accept our and others' shortcomings that we position ourselves for growth.

True Christianity is a relationship not bound by one particular religious sect or belief. We know Jesus by His words and deeds as they were recorded in the Bible. We build a personal relationship with Him when we pray and read the Bible. When we learn to see the potential and not the faults of others, we grow. When we opt to forgive and exalt our relationships rather than our hurts, we love at a fraction of how much Jesus loves us. Our goal is to learn to value and build relationships with Christ and others.

QUESTIONS

Why should we regularly attend church? There are many pastors who have been given the opportunity to teach, train, and care for the people who attend church. By attending a church, we not only hear what God is saying to His people, we are able to connect with others who can help us grow in our faith. We are all one body of believers meant to carry out a different function. Just as our physical bodies each do different things, we all have a separate job to do that offers something. When we are not there, the body does not function normally. Our church attendance does not make the church perfect, but it does help us all grow collectively and get one step closer to achieving our destinies.

Why are so many church members hypocrites? Humans by nature are not perfect and have the potential to offend, hurt, and disappoint. However, church is about our relationship with Christ. The more intimate our relationship with Christ, the more we become patient, loving, kind and accepting, and do not get offended easily. We may see people's flaws, but we choose to focus on their potential. We begin to change the environment that surrounds us. When we find a body of believers that teaches truth and meshes with our beliefs, we can't be afraid to join, begin serving, and grow as a person, thereby positively affecting our environment.

How is a spiritual relationship beneficial for my family? I noticed that when James and I thought we were "good," or able to solve our own problems, it was tougher and took longer to reach our goals. When we invited Jesus into our situations, doors opened more quickly and we made it through tough times faster. We had to learn that Jesus was the foundation that allowed us to do everything. Without Him in our lives, I shudder to think of how our lives would turn out. To gain real insight for your life, you should read the Word of

God for yourself and couple that with all the proof in your everyday surroundings.

A good example of this is the Leaning Tower of Pisa in Italy. By the time they had built three stories, they realized the foundation was not strong enough to support the building. Instead of tearing it down and starting over, they reinforced it a little more. As evidenced by time, the building began to lean and a separate structure was built near it to support its weight so it did not topple over.

Our families are similar. Unless we build a strong foundation, at some point we might ultimately have to reinforce it and hope that does the trick. Sometimes it works, and sometimes it doesn't. With Jesus as our strong foundation, we know that we will have a family built on steel reinforced pillars of concrete that will neither erode nor topple.

> *"Love comes when manipulation stops; when you think more about the other person than about his or her reactions to you. When you dare to reveal yourself fully. When you dare to be vulnerable."*
> – Dr. Joyce Brothers

NOTES:

CHAPTER 12

ANNUAL "NO KIDS ALLOWED" TRIP

"Never play peek-a-boo with a child on a long plane trip. There's no end to the game. Finally, I grabbed him by the bib and said, Look, it's always gonna be me!"

– Rita Rudner

SPOUSAL

Can you believe that my husband and I were in our early thirties before we went on our first no-kids-allowed-trip? The very first time I heard the idea, was from a couple that was returning from a seven-day excursion without their children. I was bewildered by the thought of leaving my precious and beautiful little children. I didn't think I could ever take a trip without them. They needed me, and I needed them,...or so I thought.

James and I decided to see what the excitement was all about. We chose to go on a four-day, three-night cruise to celebrate our seventh anniversary. It was long enough to make us feel like we had been away, yet not long enough to make us feel like we were having "kid withdrawal." We deemed it our "no kids allowed" trip, and off we went.

The first day we were gone, we called the kids two or three times (once we landed, before we got on the ship and before the kids' normal bed time). Day two, we called twice (when we woke up and before the kids went to sleep). Day three, we didn't call at all. Day four, we called to say we would be home shortly (right after we had planned our next getaway).

We spent the first day talking about the kids and kid-related topics because we missed hugging and kissing them. We finally decided to stop talking about them. Once we did, we relaxed and remembered life before children. Don't get me wrong, we adore our children, but we needed time apart to be with each other. We had a chance to rediscover a few things about each other that we had forgotten. From that point on, James and I made a point to plan at least two trips per year without the children.

We still do an annual family vacation and spend tons of time together. During our vacations we have driven or flown to a new city or beach we hadn't visited yet. We also enjoy staying home and doing things as a family. Sometimes we get to know the city we live in by visiting the Science Center or spending a few nights at a local hotel. We have lunch at the park, eat breakfast for dinner, hold scavenger hunts, playing board or video games, and have "sleepovers" in the living room. Whatever family activity we have planned, we enjoy ourselves immensely.

ALL-GIRLS TRIP

The second type of trip that I discovered in my early thirties was the all-girls trip. I had only seen it on television. The women would go to the resort, shop, and hang out. I had no idea that women took trips without their spouses or children. That was such a foreign concept to me. That is, until I was invited to participate in one.

This new adventure began just after moving from Texas to Arizona. During the two-month process of searching for a church, we eventually joined the Living Word Bible Church in Mesa, Arizona. This church has a phenomenal pastoral team in Doctors Tom and Maureen Anderson. We embraced the family centered activities. However, I needed something just for me. I began looking for ways to get involved with volunteer activities in hopes of befriending great women. One of the opportunities that presented itself was with a young women's Bible study group. After meeting with Pastor Kelli, I was invited to join the Daughters of Destiny ministry team. I was so excited to be asked to participate in this ministry and help its mission.

Our team met monthly to plan and prepare for each meeting. At one of those meetings, I was informed that Pastor Kelli scheduled an annual trip for all 16 of the leaders. I felt so honored because I had never been a part of anything like this before.

We went to an incredible hotel. Some of our fun included scavenger hunts, amazing meals and shopping. We bonded through teaching and prayer time. We relaxed during our spa time. Because the mission of the Living Word Bible Church is to build strong homes and families, Pastor Kelli invited the spouses and children to join us on our final day. We got to bond as a leadership group and as families. I thank Pastor Kelli for both her vision and her heart to do this for ladies.

I got to know the women in the leadership group more intimately and it cemented many friendships. It was a seed of love planted in the hearts of each team member. Because of the wonderful time I had with all of these special women, I made it a point to keep up the tradition, even after my family moved to a new city. I have organized subsequent all-girls weekend trips.

After my experiences, I suggested James create a guys-only trip. I think he is finally going to take me up on this and experience the joys of being on a trip without his wife and kids. It will be something new for him, but I think it is something he will enjoy. If anyone reading this book has a great suggestion for a "manly man's trip" (besides fishing or hunting), put it on the blog so we can help our husbands out! I think men seriously need to decompress and have some male bonding time.

<u>Here are some basic parameters for the no-kids-allowed trip</u>

1. You should plan to be gone for at least three days. Overnight stays have their place, but they are not long enough to help you appreciate all that the trip is designed to accomplish.
2. You should only call the family once in the morning and once at night. If possible, limit it to one time per day; otherwise it is as though you are not gone at all.
3. You need to plan a day of sightseeing and something relaxing. Don't forget to take lots of pictures to share with the family when you get home.
4. If it is a girls-only trip, invite no less than two friends. If it is a couples-trip, invite at least one other couple. Regardless, you should invite people with whom you have a friendship and share common interests. Plan to do a few activities together, but also plan some alone time for yourself. If that means sitting alone in the coffee shop with a cup of coffee while reading the morning paper, then do it. Just make sure that you don't need a vacation after the vacation.
5. Leave the children with someone you trust implicitly. This will lessen the anxiety of leaving them. Send the kids a postcard and pick up a souvenir or two.

6. Don't spend the entire trip talking about children; unless it is as a joke or punch line (OK, kidding about that part, but not the talking about them).
7. Before you leave, make sure to leave the kids a list of suggestions of things to do in case they get bored, and write a note letting them know that you love them.
8. If you have a disagreement with your travel mate(s), make a choice to value the relationship above the disagreement and do not allow the disagreement to carry over into the next day(s) of the trip.
9. Plan to have fun and rejuvenate yourself. Don't go away and come back the same way. Consider setting aside a morning or two for exercise.
10. Take a few minutes each day to write or read your vision. Say it out loud to yourself daily, even after you get back.

Upon your return, be prepared for a transition shock. The free buffets and maid-service will have stopped. Plan to order out at least the first night or two. If you are crafty, take the time before you leave to prepare and freeze some meals. When you return, pop it in the oven, and exhale as you eat dinner with your family.

If you can think of anything else, feel free to add it to this list. Just don't make your vacation a chore. It is meant to be a decompression time with friends or your spouse. Either way, remember to have FUN!

As I said earlier, the best thing you can do for your family is going away and taking time for yourself. The best thing you can do for your marriage, is remember what it was like in the early days and make sure to keep the love and sparks alive.

When we talk about living a life that sets an example for others, we have to incorporate time for ourselves. Few things are more precious than time. It is the only nonrenewable resource that has value in its past, present, and future. It is never selfish to do some self-preservation, except when all we are concerned about is ourselves.

PAYING FOR THE VACATION

When you are single or even before you have children, it is definitely easier to pay for vacations and make time for yourself. Once you get married and have children, it becomes more costly to prioritize vacation time. With multiple children, those concerns increase. The price for sitters or daycare can be astronomical and the opportunity to take time for you, very scarce. Regardless of your familial and financial status, it is crucial to plan time daily and through annual trips.

Trip planning requires a predetermined mind and requires you to save money, even though it may be scarce and hard to come by. In this present financial climate, "extra cash" is a seldom-heard term. However, you can still manage to eek out money to fund your trip. It may take a full year to save up an "extra" $500-$700, or you may be able to make it rather quickly. Here are a few ideas of how to pay for your trip with what you may have in your home or in your creative intellect. Check your home for items you no longer need and can sell in a yard sale. I know many women who spend their weekends buying things very inexpensively, then setting up a yard sale and refurbishing then selling the same items for a profit. If you are crafty, make something and sell it at the local weekend craft fairs. It may be tiring, but if possible, pick up an extra shift at work. If you don't want an extra shift, would you be willing to do a few odd jobs for others (sewing, ironing, cleaning, grocery shopping, or making phone calls)? It is very sacrificial, but ask your family to donate towards the trip instead of giving you Valentines, Mother's day, Christmas, or birthday gifts. However you do it, plan accordingly because it is important.

> *"Vacation used to be a luxury, but in today's world it has become a necessity."*
>
> – Author Unknown

Laundry Can Wait

NOTES:

CHAPTER 13

LOVE AND CREATE TIME FOR YOUR SPOUSE

"I've had the boyhood thing of being Elvis. Now I want to be with my best friend and my best friend is my wife. Who could ask for anything more?"
– John Lennon

I have been looking forward to this chapter the entire time I have been writing this book. I get to talk about loving my man. James and I may not be the picture perfect idea of what love entails, but I think we are growing closer by the day. I learned the value of my spouse in the tough times and then learned to appreciate him and exalt him in the good times. It was not easy, nor have we experienced all that there is to experience, but we are laying the foundation on which we can weather any storm.

The Beginning

As a matter of public record, James and I met at a network marketing business meeting in the World Trade Center. However as any married person knows, there are always two sides to the "story of how we met."

His side will probably make him look as though he was in high demand and she couldn't resist his charm. She is probably portrayed as the wide-eyed doe that fell head over heels for him.

Her side makes him look as if he couldn't resist her feminine charms, and he was immediately breathless at the sight of her. Regardless of the version rendered, the result is that the two of you managed to ultimately marry (for us married folks).

My version is going to be that James was totally smitten by me and couldn't help but to fall under my spell of allure, intelligence, beauty, and wit. So yes, I am sticking to my story, and that's all there is to it!

Laundry Can Wait

On the day of our first meeting, I spied a very handsome well-dressed young man standing in between two palm trees, taking notes and looking very suspicious. I was in charge of mingling that day and sent one of our team leaders, Noel, to draw him out of hiding. Noel was unsuccessful in her attempt. She informed me that the young man said he was a team member about to open his own office with a partner, and he wanted to take notes on how we ran our office so he could duplicate our successful environment.

This was a compliment to our team, however, he was making people nervous, so I casually glided across the room to where he was standing. I told him we needed him to use all that he had learned to that point by getting out there and assisting our team. We needed all able-bodied team members to socialize with the prospective business people gathered in the room that day. As we exchanged polite conversation, his eyes betrayed his thoughts and he appeared mesmerized, as he unsuccessfully tried to hide his bewilderment at the sight of me. I maintained my composure in the presence of this handsome man. Finally, I coaxed him into the open forum area. Reluctantly, he acquiesced but was soon saved because we were about to start the business presentation.

Interestingly enough, the very next day, about six of our team members went to Noel's house as a prelude to our office Christmas party. We were all carpooling and deciding seating arrangements when in walked James. I was shocked and slightly amused at seeing him in the house. While he and I made small talk, the team members were secretly scheming on how to get us into the same vehicle.

At the business meeting on the previous day, I had disclosed to Noel that I thought James was very handsome and I wanted to get to know him better. As Noel and the other driver, Renee, would have it, James and I not only wound up in the same car but also seated right next to each other.

At the party, James and I talked and danced all night and exchanged phone numbers to keep in touch. We discussed his living in Texas and only being in New York for seven more days to visit his parents for the Christmas holidays. Keeping his short visit in mind, we both relegated our mutual interest to that of friendship. At the time, neither James nor I wanted to get involved in a romantic relationship. At the end of the party, he said he'd call me in a few days and see if we could get together for dinner and a movie.

New York happened to be in the middle of a December snowstorm, but James didn't let a foot of snow stop him from calling me and coming to watch a movie (I told you he was smitten). In the comfort and warmth of my home, we had a great time watching a movie as we got acquainted. It was all very sweet and innocent.

Right before he left, we spent 15 minutes silently staring into each other's eyes. That was the first time I had gotten to know someone in such a short period of time and felt so connected. After that, we talked daily for at least one hour. Our longest conversation approached eight hours long. Once we each got home from work, we picked up the phone and didn't stop talking until we had to go to work the next morning. It was rough the following day, but well worth it.

We both felt it was important to build a strong foundation of friendship. It began with writing letters and escalated to huge $300 monthly phone bills. We finally progressed to flying a few times to visit each other. After a year and a half of friendship, James and I officially started dating. We had our ups and downs, but we learned the positive and negative aspects of each other's personalities.

A year after we officially began dating, I moved to Texas. It was a move I was ready to make. I had several friends and business associates warn me that I shouldn't move because they weren't sure if James and I would last. I didn't have a promise or an engagement ring. They said that I was making a horrible decision to move based off of being "in love" with James. They thought I was crazy to leave my job and city where I grew up, to go to a foreign place where I didn't know anyone except him.

They said that I was putting my trust and faith in this man and relying completely on him, and that was not wise. I admit I was hesitant about being left high and dry. Honestly, I wasn't putting my faith and trust in James. For the first time in my life, I was putting my faith and trust in Jesus. I hadn't made that decision irrationally or quickly. For several months before the move, I spent time every day in prayer figuring out if this was the right time to move and if James was *"the one."* I may have had other options from which to choose, but in my quiet time, I had a confidence and a peace that James was the one with whom I should spend my life. With that confirmation, I was able to know that it was both what I wanted, and what God wanted for me.

Now, there were many times in the past, when I wanted someone or something so bad that I convinced myself I should have what I wanted. When I look back on these decisions, I realize I made them by myself. Even when I sensed I was making the wrong choices and the clues were subtle or blatant, I never consulted God. This time, I took my time, considered all options, and invited Jesus to help me make the best decision.

A year and a half after moving to Texas, James and I got married and began our life together. Early in our marriage, we had some rocky times. Although we had a great "post honeymoon" glow about us, he was still a military intelligence officer in the US Army. James would be gone for weeks, sometimes a month or more at a time, on different training exercises. I felt like I had gotten married just to be single again.

He and I decided that we were missing too much of our life together. He wanted more from his professional life and needed to separate from the Army. As you already know, right before he discharged from the Army, I found out we were pregnant with Victoria. It was a time of excitement and trepidation as we ventured on our new life together.

Together All the Time

During this time of transition, we experienced the birth of our lovely daughter and worked our real estate investment business. What you don't know is that we subsequently purchased a pizza restaurant. We had to transition from seeing each other in the morning and evening to seeing each other ALL THE TIME! It was tough because on many days, we were at each other's throats and wanted to kick the other person out. On top of it all, we had to run a business with one assistant and several employees and then hire a restaurant manager because we couldn't be at the pizza shop.

We had different ideas on how to run a business. We disagreed on everything from how much to pay employees to what skills we required in them. The first six months of our entrepreneurial adventure, we mixed professional with personal and it was a disaster. Oh, by the way, I was pregnant and had some serious hormones raging. We worked hard at living out our spiritual and moral values while still being shrewd business owners. Sometimes we failed miserably, and other times we excelled and were great examples of teamwork. We had to learn to find the correct balance between personal and business.

After the pizza restaurant experiment failed, our financial standing and rental properties faltered and caused many other financial ripples. We had to use our rental property income to offset some of the bad debt owed on the restaurant. Not only had we made poor financial decisions, we had a period where we didn't agree on any course of action and were bitter towards each other. Being newlyweds and new parents who didn't spend much quality time together, only compounded matters. To make matters worse, we had no real down time apart to sort out our emotions and thoughts. We spent all day at the office together and then we rode home and were at home together.

To add fuel to the growing inferno of financial woes, our accountant told James he needed to get a traditional job to rebuild his credit, or we would soon have nothing but bankruptcy as a result. Our financial situation was dire, and our family was under tremendous stress. It was a tough pill to swallow. We had to take any income we earned from the rental properties and real estate sales to pay employees. We barely had enough to keep a roof over our heads and food on our table. We had an ever-growing mountain of debt, and all we had worked for to that point was about to take a nosedive.

I remember days when I thought, "I want a divorce. This is not what I bargained for. I can do bad all by myself!" Thankfully, before we got married, James and I discussed and agreed that divorce was not an option for us. We vowed to work through anything. It took a while for the "frost" in our lives to melt, but the point is that it melted.

It was not until we sat down and talked, yelled, cried, and faced the situation that we were able to help each other heal our wounds. It may not have been what either of us bargained for that early on in our marriage, but it was a good test that taught us many powerful lessons. If we neglected each other and didn't communicate, we would always be surrounded by commotion.

From that point forth, the four action steps that guided us in business and personal matters were to put our thoughts before God and ask the Lord to show us our hearts. We wanted to make sure that we were not putting our selfish desires ahead of the good of the marriage and family.

Step 1: *Prayer:* "God I have these feelings and issues that I want to bring to You. Help me address them with my spouse. If I am being selfish in any way, please show it to me right now so that I can correct that within myself and be a better person.

If we were putting selfish desires first, we asked the Lord to show us our errors so we could discuss it with our spouse.

Step 2: *Action:* You have to allow God to show you the good, bad and ugly.

After that, we asked God to make our conversation with our spouse productive by allowing our spouse to "hear" the true intent of the person speaking.

Step 3: *Prayer 2:* "God, now that I have dealt with my hurts, rejections, thoughts, and emotions, please allow me to effectively communicate these to my spouse in a way that they will best receive what I am saying. Please allow their heart to understand that I love them and want to see our marriage grow. In Jesus' name, Amen."

We sat down, talked with the spouse, took notes, and shared all of our thoughts. We restated what the other said to make sure that we were not hearing something contrary to what the spouse attempted to communicate.

Step 4: *Honesty:* Have the conversation with your spouse while being tactful, yet honest.

This is a working model of how we do things. We have learned that when we invite God into our conversations BEFORE we talk with each other, we always get better results. Without our faith in God, we would never make it. For us, we only know Christ the King, and we put Him at the forefront of our marriage. We truly believe that this is how we are able to pass through storms relatively unscathed.

My Best Friend

Since we began dating, James has been my best friend. There were times early on when he had to compete with others for my time and attention, and I felt disloyal to my long-standing friendships by spending so much time with him. When he was around, I felt like one of those girls who hides themselves away and gets completely lost in being with her guy. When he wasn't around, I felt like I had to make up for lost time with my other friends to make them feel like I was giving them my attention. I just couldn't figure out the balance.

I thought I had to give 100% of my attention to each friendship, and I felt guilty for not being able to comply. It finally dawned on me that I didn't have to. That was a revelation to me because I have always been an all-or-nothing type person. I figured out we could do group outings that incorporated our core groups of friends. Some friends were very accepting of these outings, while others came grudgingly or not at all. It became apparent to some of my friends that we were no longer in sync as friends, and we eventually stopped hanging out.

This was an uneasy, hurtful part of my life. I was reminded of the poem by Charlsy Soccer Chick: "People come into my life for a reason, a season, or a lifetime."[10] I hang onto those lifetime friends with vigor, and the seasonal friends are highly regarded, while the reason friends come and go. I am prepared for all and gladly accept them into my life. As I get older, I am learning to cultivate lifetime friendships and nurture seasonal friendships.

The most pervasive lifetime friendship that I can cultivate is one of mutual respect and commitment with my husband. He is always there and we go through everything together. Like traditional friendships, we have to foster it. We have to spend time together in order for us to grow. We have to encourage each other and pick each other up when life hands us situations that may momentarily knock us down. We have to be willing to lock arms and stand firm against every adversity. Sometimes, we are our own worst enemies because we allow ourselves to think the worst and act upon a lie. As we create a solid friendship, we are able to uncover the truth of situations more quickly. Sometimes the truth hurts, but that is where love and respect have a hand.

Part of loving each other as friends means that we are honest and don't lie. Not even a little lie. That can be hard, especially when it comes to silly questions like, "Honey, do I look fat in this outfit?" In all honesty, I was tying my husband's hand. I said I wanted the truth, but I couldn't handle the truth and didn't really want to hear the truth. I have since learned not to ask those types of questions but rather to ask how an outfit looks on me.

A lie is the small unraveling of trust that leads to breakdowns in every aspect of friendship and marriage. You may think you are saving your spouse from some terrible end, but what you are really doing is undermining your standing in their eyes and lowering their ability to trust you. A lie is not worth the sacrifice that is caused.

Another part of friendship is learning to live, love, and laugh together in any situation. Think about a good female friend. When you think about her, you may think about the funny things that happened while you were together or the best laugh you ever had with her.

As with that friend, you should have similar types of interactions with your spouse, except much more intimately. You should always be able to think of a time you enjoyed each other's company. Reminisce about a time that warms your heart. Can you think of a time when something silly happened? Do you have any private or public jokes that only the two of you understand? If you can't reference any of these, you should seriously consider getting started on creating a foundational friendship with your spouse. It is in the tough times of marriage that the choice of friendship will help ground the choice of love.

The most touching thing my husband has ever said to me was, "You inspire me to greatness!" It had a great impact on me because my very accomplished husband expressed one of my heart's desires for him. Even though he has others who are equally qualified to motivate him, I took great pride in knowing that I was inspiring him. Although it should not have been a surprise for me to hear these words, it was. Inspiring him is something that I have always endeavored to do; it was comforting and sobering to hear it spoken. Often times, those we care about suffer from familiarity and forget to say the words that most affect one another's lives. It was in this one instance that my life was transformed. James pushed me to achieve even greater things so that I could prove him right.

Correct Perspective

Having the correct perspective about loving and creating time for your spouse can be a challenge. As women, we are pulled in so many different directions that we hardly have time for ourselves, much less time for our spouse. I remember, early on in our marriage, James and I would sit by the fireplace and play games or talk. Once the children came into the picture, that happened less frequently, OK, maybe it stopped happening altogether. I got so caught up in being a mother that I forgot about being a wife. James was getting the short end of the stick, yet I kept pulling that stick asking him to help me.

I'll go back to the example of the bank. I kept making withdrawals from him emotionally and physically, yet I wasn't putting as much back into him to replenish his "love tank."[11] I asked him to watch the baby while I napped. He had to go to work. He helped cook when I didn't get around to it. The house still needed to be cleaned and the baby bathed. At times, I told him I didn't have time to play games or make love because all I wanted to do was sleep. I neglected my poor husband in lieu of sleep and in pursuit of my learning how to be a mother. My rationale was simple: since we lived in the same house, it was not unreasonable for me to ask for his help. I mean, I worked just as hard as he did, and even harder because I worked 24/7 without a break. I thought I was entitled to help and saw little need to reciprocate.

Entitlement is what every mom believes is her right once she has to carry, deliver, and raise a child. To a certain extent, we are entitled to help, but that help will come at a high cost if we continue to use the people around us. Everyone deserves to be treated with respect. A simple "thank you" goes a long way to filling the "love tank" of a spouse.

Call your hubby to say, "Hi, honey, I just wanted to let you know I was thinking of you." It will put a smile on your spouse's face.

An "I want you to know that I really appreciate all you do for our family" makes a world of difference and builds up your husband's confidence level.

Don't get me wrong, women contribute a ton to the working of the family. However, acknowledgement of all that others do to allow us to do what we do is always appreciated. Hug your hubby once he walks in the door. Drop a love note in his briefcase, or even make your spouse's favorite meal and tell him you thought of him that day.

Correct perspective is about putting the time in to create a strong foundation so that, as you grow older, you and your spouse grow together, not apart, and you lay the groundwork for life after children. And yes, there is life after children.

Enroll In The Vision

One of the best things I ever learned to do was to accept James' help and not force him to do things my way. I am a very particular person who likes things done a certain way, so this took lots of patience and deep breathing on my part. I don't always think my way is best, but most times, it is (just kidding). I had to let him discover what was best for him so he would enjoy contributing to the family.

I remember, early on, I would make the bed a certain way and he would make his side a different way. I would ask him why he tucked the sheets that way and he quoted his military training. I couldn't argue with that, so I left it alone. I asked why he squeezed the toothpaste from the top of the tube, rather than the bottom; he had no real answer, so I would squeeze it up from the bottom and fill in the dent he made at the top. I asked why he put the toilet tissue roll with the flap side up versus down, and he could only answer that is how he grew up doing it. Lots of minute, unimportant issues, but how we handled them made a world of difference.

We learned how each of us responded to different situations. Our responses were a good indication of how we would respond when the bigger things happened. We had to figure out how to diagnose a sick child. Would we call the in-laws or call the medical help line? How would we handle a financial crisis?

If we misspoke and said something with a perceived harsh tone, our message was met with mild irritation. If we were relating our hopes and dreams for the future with the word "I," and not "we," the wrong message was sent. We continually strove to accept each other's viewpoints by effectively communicating.

By having two different visions in a marriage, neither one will be completed with much success. By creating one unified vision of expectations, there is a greater chance of reaching milestones quickly while establishing new visions for the future. It's like when we were children running the three-legged race. If both partners learned to run with the tied legs as one leg, they can run fast and win. If one person wants to be more dominate and runs faster, not only do they fall, somebody gets hurt in the process. The same concept applies to our visions.

If you want a hubby who will love being involved as a dad, husband, and helper to you, please do not limit him by forcing him to always do it your way. Your spouse is not the extra child and should never be treated that way. If your hubby feels this way, he may quickly "check out" and relegate all things to you. You risk stifling and limiting the fatherly effect your husband has on the children and the husbandly effect he has with you. He may be there physically, but not available mentally. He may find time to do other things that don't involve you or the children. It is a subtle mistake, but one that many of us women have made at one point or another. As a loving friend and wife, it is up to you to build a life with your spouse and children.

When Victoria and Jimmy were younger, I made life all about them, and sometimes I would involve James in what we were doing. I would have "family time with mom," and then inform James he could participate if he wanted. This was backwards because I was building a family without involving him. I didn't see it at the time, but thankfully, James loved me enough to let me know I was leaving him out of his family! I was doing it unintentionally, but nevertheless, I was doing it.

I had to consciously incorporate James into everything we did. I would ask him to plan family outings or some of our weekly family nights. I would plan to do things that he enjoyed doing. I would encourage the kids to ask dad for help and not always come to me. We didn't have family time unless dad was around. I made my husband a major part of the family, and I am so glad that I did. He now enjoys his dominant role in our family and has stepped into it like never before.

I had to stop being the stereotypical strong, independent woman who could do it all by myself. I had to learn that even though I *could* do it by myself, it was out of order because I had a spouse who desperately wanted to join in. Just as much as I had wanted to be a strong mom, he wanted to be a strong dad. Once I opened what I deemed as "my family," I saw a different side of him. It became "our family," and he has grown into a nurturing, doting man whom our children are fortunate to have as a father and I appreciate having as a husband.

I think that I am the one who is reaping the most benefits. I get to see him grow as a man and every day he is displaying character traits of what I have always wanted in a husband, father, and man. He is my all and my everything. I'm growing into the woman I desire, because he has given me the freedom to discover myself.

My vision for being a balanced woman is intertwined with my goals for our family. As a wife, I am building a strong and supportive foundation with my dear husband. Our family may change over time, but at its core are things that never change: love and unity.

Be the Example

If you take one thought from this book, it is, "Parent with the end in mind." When you love, respect, enjoy, and are friends with your spouse, it establishes a strong marriage and sets the example for your children.

I remember growing up watching shows like *The Cosby Show, Married With Children, The Brady Bunch, Little House on the Prairie, Family Ties, Good Times, The Jefferson's,* and *Fresh Prince of Bel Aire*, that showed the dynamics of different families. As I said, I remember being keenly aware of how my family was different from most of the television families I saw portrayed on television. I grew up in a single-parent household, so I couldn't relate to many of the shows where two parents were present, but that didn't stop me from dreaming about having two parents in my house.

I almost idolized some of the shows that displayed a successful couple with well-rounded children and a loving home environment. I wished that were my house, and I was a part of their family. Alas, I realized that everything was not like the television shows. I learned quite a lot by living in my home environment, and I formed ideas of what I wanted my life to be like when I grew up and had a family of my own.

I believe that seeing positive examples of different family environments helped me to form my prospective parenting style and learn to set a good example. I remember one day when the children were watching television, one of them said, "Mom and Dad, our family is more fun than theirs." I know a little bit of hubris, but to know that my children find identity and joy in being members of our family is a badge of honor.

I love that they would rather play games, read, go on walks, cook, or go out as a family than watch television or do things with their friends. I get excited when we plan our annual family vacation and the kids chime in with where they've been or what they enjoyed doing. It makes me feel great.

Just to be clear, the comparison is not out of high-minded conceit. It is from the joy and identity the kids get from being a part of our family. It is the same pride as when a parent comments on how much they love our children, or how well behaved and respectful our children are around adults. It gives us an inward feeling that we are doing something right.

As a family unit, James and I make a point to show the children how our family remains strong. We consistently display love towards each other by going on dates. When James and I go on dates without the children, we make sure they know we are going on a date. We let them know when we are going away for the night or weekend because we love each other and need to spend time together. This is how husbands and wives learn to be best friends and love each other more over time. They often whine about us leaving, but in reality they love it when we go without them. When we get back from our date, we share some of the things we did, because we know they enjoy hearing about it. They love to see us dance in the middle of the kitchen or hug when we pass each other in the hall. They enjoy watching us be silly or competitive at games

The children have a regularly scheduled bedtime and we enforce it with vigor. We let them know that it is time for them to go to bed because they need extra sleep and Mom and Dad need to spend time together. James even jokes that by 7:45PM (school nights), if the kids are still awake, he starts to develop a twitch in his neck. He begins to move as fast as an Indy Car driver to get them to bed. Because this time is coveted and deemed, our time we don't want it to be interrupted.

When we inform them of these things, we are including them in the loving part of our marriage. We are modeling for them the expectation that as parents, you do things to build the other up. We are sharing with them that we love them, but that we also love each other.

We don't engage in "disagreeable discussions" in front of them, but they are aware when we may have issues. We respect them enough to not have certain discussions in front of them (adult-related content). If they catch us on the cusp of a disagreement, they say, "We love you Mom and Dad. Don't get upset." When we disagree, we model how to have a civil discussion, or we table it for later if we feel it is not getting resolved.

They know that Mom and Dad love each other and have fun together. They know that we love them beyond measure. We know we are doing a good job when they say, "When I grow up, I want to be like Mom and Dad and have three children." Make it a point to love your child, and show them the qualities of a loving relationship so as they grow up, they will expect only the best and have formidable standards for a "friend" or spouse.

James and I plan many types of date nights. One long weekend, I asked my mother to keep the kids for the night and I surprised James with an overnight date night. I reserved a room at a local hotel and packed us a bag for the night. I found out the times of a movie theater near the hotel and planned to have dinner and dessert at a nearby restaurant. He had absolutely no idea and it was wonderful.

This may appear lavish and cost-prohibitive, but I spent $59 for the two-day excursion, including the hotel. The good thing is that James had accrued hotel points, and we used one night's worth. The hotel was virtually free, whereas it might have cost upwards of $150 per night. If you decide to go this route, go to one of the travel sites and book a low cost room for as little as $39/night for a three-five star hotel. The whole idea should be to make it a night all about him. I don't really like going out to movie theaters, but I love James and he enjoys it, so we did what I thought he would enjoy.

On another date night, it cost me $15 and involved, dancing, tapas (appetizers), and a small basket of love. I looked in the local entertainment section of the "upcoming things to do in my town" and found a free dance lesson being hosted by a local dance school. I registered over the phone. I prepared a theme-based picnic for him. It was raining that night, but the location was under an outdoor park pavilion with picnic tables. After the lesson, I spread out the tablecloth, unloaded the basket of goodies and we feasted on various crackers, breads, and dips. I bought a frozen tiramisu dessert, made some iced coffees and juice spritzers. It was so much fun, and we had an incredible time of tango, romance, and food. Afterwards, the dance school's director came over to us and told us that she had never seen anything so upscale, yet simple and romantic.

These are just two ideas of what you can do to have a romantic evening. Search local resources (newspapers, magazines, and websites) to find free or low-cost things to do. Make an effort to plan something you want to do, and then allow your spouse to plan something he wants to do. By doing this, you are both sharing your interests and joys with each other and helping your spouse to know your interests.

Single Parenting

If you don't have a spouse or significant other, learn to love YOURSELF! Spend time developing a hobby or deepening friendships. Figure out what you want out of life. I know that mothers have a tendency to go all-out and give their all to their children. The downside to doing this is that if you give your child your all, what do you have left for you? You are the most important person in that child's life, and you need to remind yourself that you are valuable. I am not insinuating that you shouldn't love your child with your all; you should. It is your responsibility to love and nurture the child that was created inside of you. You also have the duty to yourself. You can't lose your identity as a woman because of your role as a mom.

As a product of a single-parent household, I learned that I had to be strong no matter what. I discovered that with hard work and discipline, I could achieve great things. I learned that my mother would do just about anything for us. My mother is a testament to women everywhere and I saw the effects of how hard it was to raise five children all by herself.

I also witnessed my mother's lonely and weary days where she wished she had help, but the help available didn't meet all of her needs. It's tough for children to watch their mother be sad or hurt. Children only want love and happiness for their parents, and when you work to do that for yourself, you are securing love in the heart of your children. Ladies, don't underestimate the effect you have in your child's life. It may seem that what you say goes in one ear and out the other, but something is sticking and will eventually help them to grow into strong, independent people.

In setting the example for your daughter, decide what example you want her to follow as she grows up. It is also important to model an example of the type of woman your son will date and ultimately marry. Are you showing your children that you respect yourself by taking care of your needs? If not, you have to be their example.

You love them by tending to them when they are younger. As they grow older, you empower them. When Victoria was four and Jimmy was three, I taught them how to sort and fold laundry. Certainly tedious, but it was fun for them and allowed them to feel like they were helping me. When Victoria was six and Jimmy was five, they learned how to bathe themselves unassisted. When Victoria was seven and Jimmy was five and a half, they learned how to do basic chores such as cleaning their bathroom mirrors, taking out the trash and cleaning their sinks.

As a child, I was given these tasks. When I was 10, I learned how to cook for the family. It is my belief that every child should be responsible for assisting the family with something around the house. Chores build children's confidence and their identity as family members. It could be as simple as helping put all the toys away or as complex as preparing the family's meals. Whatever you decide, make it something that helps the family.

Now, here's a warning, don't immediately correct or re-do what the children have done. Inspect their work, but allow them to fix it to the standard you desire. Make sure to praise their efforts. If after checking their initial results, it is still not done to your standard, wait until sometime later to re-do it.

At first, it takes longer to do it this way than to do it yourself; but in the end, you are educating and creating self-sufficient children who will be able to master life skills and tasks when they grow up. The best part of this whole thing is the children feel empowered, trusted, and released to be active, productive, helpful family members. Your involvement of them in the workload of the family helps them find identity and joy. It also allows you some extra time to concentrate on doing other things.

Help yourself by teaching others how best and most effectively to help you. When you allow others to do this, they love on themselves and appreciate you.

> *"If a man truly wants to communicate with his wife, he must enter her world of emotions."*
> – Gary Smalley

NOTES:

PART 3
LIVE FOR TODAY

CHAPTER 14

BE A PLANNER WHO PLANS SPONTANEITY!!

> "Bad planning on your part does not constitute an emergency on my part."
>
> – Proverb

Oxymoron or Not?

I know it seems like a weird title, but this section is about scheduling and how you have to plan time to be spontaneous. I am a planner, so I can speak from my experience that in order to have fun, sometimes I have to plan nothing. Sometimes I have to ditch the plan all together. If you look at the schedule below, you will see one of my typical weekly calendars. Note the areas that are intentionally left blank. These are my areas of spontaneity. I do not plan things to do during that time, except, maybe something restful or fun. On occasion, I even leave it up to someone else to plan.

I normally have time to do other things while Ella takes a nap or while I wait for the kids to get done with gymnastics practice. I schedule free time during the weekends, but I also make time during the week. When we have time, we like to conduct scavenger hunts, play games, have family reading time, or art projects.

I've said this before, but I think it has to be repeated. Reserve time with your spouse after the children go to bed. Spend time talking or doing something constructive with your hubby. Sometimes, we do nothing, and that works well too. Because we have decided that the children go to bed at a certain time, it frees us up to do what we need to do for our night, or the next day.

	Sunday	Monday	Tuesday	Wednesday	Thursday	Friday	Saturday
6-7		Wake/workout	Wake/workout	Wake/workout	Wake/workout	Wake/workout	Wake/Workout
7-8	Wake up	B-fast	B-fast	B-fast	B-fast	B-fast	
8-9	Breakfast	School	School	School	School	School	B-fast
9-10	Church	Sesame St.	Sesame St.	Sesame St.	Sesame St.	Sesame St.	Bible Study
10-11	Church	Learning w/Ella	Fun/park	Learning w/Ella	Fun/park	Fun/park	Chores
11-12	Lunch	Lunch	Lunch	Lunch	Lunch	Lunch	
12-1		Nap-Ella	Nap-Ella	Nap-Ella	Nap-Ella	Nap-Ella	Lunch
1-2			Laundry	Cleaning	Write	Write	
2-3		Study	Laundry				
3-4	Dinner prep	Pick up kids	Pick up kids	Pick up kids	Gymnastics	Pick up kids	
4-5		Dinner prep	Dinner prep	Dinner prep	Gymnastics	Dinner prep	
5-6	Dinner	Gymnastics	Dinner	Dinner	Dinner	Dinner	Dinner
6-7	Baths-kids	Gymnastics	Class-Dee	Bath-kids	Bath-kids	Family time	
7-8	Bed	Bed	Bed	Bed	Bed	Family time	
8-9	James/Dee	James/Dee	James/Dee	James/Dee	James/Dee	James/Dee	DateNite

Learn To Let Go

Before I got married and had children, I was able to plan my life out to the minute, and it went relatively as expected. As someone who was intimately tied to a schedule, it was hard for me to understand why arranging things with my husband and children did not go as I had planned. It was hard for me to recalibrate from one mindset to another. Once I became the COO of Personal Development and

Operations, I became effective at home schooling the children. I learned the differences in each child's learning style, and I was able to teach them simultaneously.

While initially home schooling the children, I planned our day in 30-minute increments with specific work to be completed. Every 30 minutes, we were supposed to do a different activity. I kept wondering why our day kept going off schedule and we were not getting much accomplished.

During that time, I discovered that Victoria was time conscious, and she wanted to know how long we were going to do an activity. She wanted to use her time effectively. Jimmy was more activity-based. He wanted to choose which activity was most fun so he could spend more time on that one. It was frustrating because some activities lingered while others we breezed through.

I finally had a heart-to-heart with myself and changed how I thought about time. I worked to become effective with both children and maintain control of our day. I decided that we would be activity-focused with a flexible time constraint attached. That way, Victoria would know how much time she had for any activity, and Jimmy would be able to pick what he wanted to work on first and not feel rushed.

I eliminated much of my frustration by letting go of my rigid schedule and adapting to our circumstances. I learned to tweak my teaching style to that of my children's way of learning. Once I figured out the trick, we had a very productive year.

After Victoria went to kindergarten and Jimmy was alone with me at home, I had to focus on him. I allowed him to choose what we did first. We were able to be flexible with how long any one activity lasted.

Now that both children are in school and I am alone with Ella, I have to adjust my schedule again. Originally, I was nervous at the thought of being home alone with one child. I had two children at home for such a long time, I thought I would be bored and not have much to do. Boy, was I wrong!

Ella's personality is very alert, and she is very advanced, which forces me to constantly expose her to new things. She loves to go anywhere. She gets cabin fever if she is in the house for more than a few hours. I love her desire to get up and always go, but at times, it's hampered by her nap schedule, which is in the process of changing. She, in her infinite two-year-old wisdom, has informed me that she doesn't take naps anymore. I laugh because she is the same age Victoria and

Jimmy decided they were done with naps. However, I don't think I am quite ready to give up my personal time that I have become accustomed to experiencing. I think quiet time is about to be instituted and hopefully she can appreciate some quiet time instead of nap time.

As part of letting go, I rediscovered how enjoyable eating breakfast for dinner could be. I used to eat this way in college, but I didn't believe this alternative was an appropriate meal to serve to my family at dinnertime. However, my family now has an affinity for this dinner option. Victoria started it one year as a birthday dinner request. (I always make the birthday person their favorite meal.) I could not contain my enthusiasm as I agreed, and made her feel special. Since then, I make breakfast for dinner as a special treat, and everyone enjoys it. I have let go of many mental blocks regarding what is and is not appropriate.

In special unplanned moments, our family likes to commit random acts of fun or love. This translates to a hug while making dinner or dancing while making the table. My personal favorite is doing something silly behind someone's back. We attempt to keep the mood of our household light and full of joy. We don't always take things seriously. Since our family members are competitive creatures, as far as sports and games, we love to encourage the person who wins. However, this is fuel for everyone to practice until they can unseat the other party and then gloat about the accomplishment. A few times, too much gloating has cost the other person cool points when they were kicked out of first place abruptly. The key is not to get jealous or overly competitive. All is fair in love and family game playing!

Windows of Opportunity

There will be windows of opportunity opening in the lives of your family that are totally spontaneous. You need to be keenly aware of and take full advantage of them by making a strong connection. These windows of opportunity will be a call for you to enter the private thoughts of your child or spouse. It can come across as a simple statement that invites you into a conversation or a topic that is acutely interesting to that person. It could come as a repeated, "Mom come look at this," or "Mom guess what?" or even, "Honey, I was thinking..." These statements are not always the "in" you may be looking for, but you should keep your ears open to them so that you don't miss out on a critical point.

On one occasion, I became the best mom ever, in the eyes of Victoria. We were preparing to go shopping for a few groceries. She was playing dress-up and had on her princess outfit. I informed her that we had to go and she would have to change, resulting in a mini-meltdown. I was getting annoyed. To smooth things over and get out the house, I smiled and said, "Stop crying because a princess can't go anywhere with wet eyes and tears streaming down her face." She looked up at me with wide-eyed amazement, "You mean I can wear my princess dress and shoes? I love you so much Mom! Thank you."

I initially did it to calm her down so we could get out the door. However, it was at that moment that I stepped into her fantasy world and became the best mom in the whole world, or better yet, universe. After all, she was fully-clothed and looked absolutely adorable. As we made our way down the aisles of the grocery store, people stared. Some had the disapproving face of, "How can you let your child come out of the house in play clothes?" Others smiled and asked her if she was going to a ball because she was the prettiest princess they had ever seen. She said she was playing and having the best day ever.

My heart lit up and I smiled at the adoring fans (and at the disapproving ones). No matter what people said or how they looked at us, I was my child's hero for the day. Victoria knew this wouldn't happen all the time, but she did ask a few other times. Most times, she had to change, but this one time, it was not worth fighting, and it brought more joy to our hearts in the moments we shared being queen and princess!

One of James' open windows came when we were talking and he needed me to listen to his thoughts without comment. He was perplexed by choices he had to make about switching employers and position within the new company. He shared his heart and mind and was inviting me to silently help him sort through this situation. He needed me to be a sounding board, but not solve his problem for him. My silence allowed him the ability to think and talk through different scenarios.

Other times, he needed me to comment and have a bilateral conversation. Sometimes I asked questions to probe deeper thought. Occasionally, I offered different solutions to his problems. Whatever he needs, I step in to maintain our close communication.

When talking, we always ask what role we need the other to play. Do we want silence or do we want help to find a solution? This lets the other party know what role is needed of them. Sometimes the conversations were planned out, and other times, it was 10pm and we were lying in bed with no forethought that we were about to embark on a three-hour conversation.

No matter how it manifests, the goal is to show your spouse that you are open to hearing his heart whenever he needs to talk. If there is a point where you have been offended or have hurt your spouse, you run the risk of either closing yourself off from a window of opportunity or missing one entirely. This is a difficult situation because you can leave a void where a loving moment had the potential to exist. There is no better way to fill your spouse's "love tank" than by making him feel that you are available and ready to listen to his heart.

Whether you are working to establish a relationship with your family or friends, look for windows of opportunities in both their conversations and actions. It will enhance your relationship with that person and build value. If you miss a window, don't beat yourself up over it; for a new opportunity may present itself soon thereafter. Just make sure you are ready the next time.

> *"Expect the best, plan for the worst, and prepare to be surprised."*
>
> – Denis Waitley

NOTES:

CHAPTER 15

FALL IN LOVE WITH BEING A MOM

"To accomplish great things, we must not only act, but also dream; not only plan, but also believe."
– Anatole France

One of the foundational truths about being a mom is understanding that no matter what happens in your child's life, it is simply a stage they are experiencing. No child will remain Terrifically Two, Interestingly Tween, or Soon-to-be-Eighteen forever. You can ask any mom who is or has raised a child; she will undoubtedly tell you she misses a particular stage of her child's life. I personally miss the days of toothless smiles, immobile grinning babies looking at me with wide-eyed amazement as they figured out life, bath time with little wriggly wet bodies and rubber ducky toys, and the days where all it took was my kiss to make everything all better. On the opposite end of the spectrum, the things I am glad to be done with are: sleepless nights, potty training, not understanding what my children were saying, especially when they were sick or hurt, and screaming toddlers thrashing about on the floor wanting special attention (that is, until the next baby comes along).

In the first few years of parenting, I wish I had an understanding of how quickly life moments would happen. I had no appreciation of how cherished a memory would be until my hard drive crashed and we lost many of Victoria's first-year baby pictures. I had no understanding of how much of the baby stage I enjoyed until my children grew out of it and headed to new ground. I had no real grasp of how the personalities of children changed so dramatically from baby to toddler to adolescent to teen until my teenage sister grew up. I blinked and missed her youth.

I wonder how my early parenting persona ultimately affected the way my children have developed. I reflect on some of the mistakes I made, and if they were as detrimental as I had envisioned them to be. I muse on how I could have allowed precious time to fly by as a bystander who watched it all drift away. I speculate about times when I could have started affecting the lives of my children so that their tomorrows would not only be a treasure for them, but for me as well.

Then I exhale, and realize that yesterday is gone and tomorrow is not promised, but today is a gift, and that is why it is called the present. I can wonder all I want or beat myself up over the past, but what good is that going to do in my affecting my today or tomorrow? If I am going to enjoy being a mom and absolutely love this part of my life, I have to stop wasting time with *"what if?"* I have to focus on *right now* and what I am doing to live a fulfilled, joyful life. I ask you to make the same type of declaration I made a few years ago.

Today, I, (insert your name here), choose to be a fantastic mom who loves every minute of being a mom. It may not always be easy or comfortable. I may have tough days and days where I don't feel like being in love with being a mom, but I CHOOSE to enjoy every aspect of it and find the joy in the moment. I am the best mom in the whole wide world for my child, (insert name here). I love, (insert child's name here) and will do my best to learn from the past, live for today and have a vision for the future.

By making this declaration, you are focusing on the present and future while learning from past mistakes. You are choosing to declare that no matter what happens, you are working to be a great mom who makes wise choices. You are committing to walking out your desire to have a vision for your family. You are acknowledging the reality of situations yet choosing to focus on the positive aspects.

One day last year, I was forced to stop in my tracks and remember why I love being a mom. I call it "Little Blue Socks."

I went about the day as normal, doing the things that needed to get done. You know, laundry, making meals, cleaning, playing with the kids, and weaning Ella off the bottle to the cup, grocery shopping, and all the other things I can't remember right now. At the end of the day, I walked into the bedroom as I prepared to shower. Just before I stepped into the shower, I opened my closet door, wondering why it was closed in the first place. I looked into my closet to ensure my dress had not fallen down and was ready for church on Sunday morning. I was met with two racks of shoes spread out all over the closet floor. Irritated, I got in the shower and wondered why in the world the bedroom door was left open and why one of the children got into the closet and started playing with my shoes. My initial thought centered on Ella, and now I was going to have to clean it all up. Could I really be upset with a little 21-month-old toddler?

As the water cascaded down my body and I relaxed, I forgot about the shoes and what awaited me once I was finished. After getting out of the shower and preparing myself for bed, I walked past the closet and realized that I still needed to clean up the shoes. I got down on my knees and started sorting shoes, grumbling about always having to clean up after the kids. I saw something that stopped me in my tracks. I saw two little blue socks underneath a pair of my favorite high-heeled shoes. The first thought was: A-ha, it was Ella and my suspicion of her being the culprit behind the great shoe caper was solved! A wellspring of emotion flooded my heart, and a fountain of tears rolled down my cheeks as I sat relishing in the moment. Smiling, I yelled to James, "I guess Ella loves my shoes, too!"

This moment represented one of the journeys of being a mom and absolutely loving it. In the midst of the mess and clean up, all I could picture was the love in her eyes and joy in her heart as she pulled, tried on, and discarded pair after pair of shoes until she found the ones that Mommy really liked. I saw her standing up and wobbling while she wore the shoes. I saw her standing up, walking with her hands out, smiling, and her curly hair bobbing up and down. She pretended to be Mom and loved every minute of it. I heard her clicking around on the floor while she shook her hips and "boo-tay," singing the "ABCs" or "Twinkle Twinkle Little Star" to her hearts content. I enjoyed looking at the mess with the little blue socks in the middle of it all. Now, whenever I see a mess, I see those little blue socks and realize that nothing is as big of a mess as I think.

To be honest, I left the socks sitting right there in the middle of the closet floor for nearly two weeks. I needed a daily reminder of how much my children love me and how they show it in unconventional ways. As a result, I smiled more and created an environment that fostered joy and peace.

Little blue socks mean the love of a child for a parent and a parent's joy at seeing their children want to be like them. I adore being a mom. I especially enjoy my children and all their little blue-sock moments.

The Process of Motherhood

Can you truthfully admit that, before you became a mother, you did not understand that motherhood was a process? I count myself

Laundry Can Wait

among the many people who thought there was somehow a mommy gene that instinctively kicked in and showed us all how to be great moms. I love kids and used to babysit quite often, so by all practical accounts, I had real-life experience.

Well, nothing quite prepared me for what I would experience, or the fact that I was growing by leaps and bounds in my mommy voyage. Yes, some things automatically kicked in. However, just as we learned the fundamentals of math in school and built upon them until we were able to do more complex math, so is our journey as moms. To be the best we can be, we have to invest energy and be teachable. Not every program or book is right for us, but we have to go through the steps to determine what we can and can't use.

The process of motherhood is lined with detours, bumps, hurts, and plenty of happiness. We have growing pains and a learning curve from the outset. Even as seasoned moms, we have to relearn what we discovered in error or were never taught.

One area of the process involves having unreal expectations that even a supermom can't achieve. Don't beat yourself up if you aren't able to do everything in one day. It's difficult to be in several places at once. Fret not if you can't bake a batch of homemade cookies with milk, for when the kids come home. The key is to find a way to share individual time with each child to make them feel special. You will have to evenly rotate your affection. Take turns hugging each child while you read them a story. Allow each of your children to help prepare dinner or dessert. You can orchestrate weekly dates with each of your children. The dates can be as simple as taking them out for ice cream or lunch.

The other side of expectations is not having any, but parenting from day-to-day. Part of the process involves you discovering who you are and defining your particular mommy style. Don't allow life to pass you by because you are consumed with your daily activities. Choose to actively participate and let your children know that you are there for them when they need you. Don't fall prey to, "Well, my parents didn't do that, so I shouldn't do that either." This is your parenting journey: don't be afraid to experience it to the fullest. Take the good memories, fuse them with your personality, and create great new experiences for your children.

I, like many moms I know, wish my role as a mom was easy. Unfortunately, it is far from easy. It is hard work. I often tell people that the most arduous, yet rewarding job I have ever chosen was becoming a stay-at-home-mother. I did not fully understand the time commitment, personality triggers, and vast amounts of energy that I would have to expend in my daily walk as a mom. It is a 24-hour, seven-day per week job, 365 days a year (366 on leap year)! There are few breaks and even family vacations are work. Still, there is much fun to be had during all the work. First I had to stop seeing it as work and start seeing it as an opportunity to build relationships with some of the most important people I would ever know.

Understand that the process to becoming a great mom is not a sprint to a final destination. It is more of a marathon. It is a journey that takes everything within you and then requires you give more. You have to endure through it all not just by living, but by making a concerted effort to embrace and enjoy the process. The amount of training that goes into preparation for the big race is what distinguishes the finishers from those that quit.

During a marathon, I am told, that your lungs burn, your body hurts uncontrollably, and you are driven to pure exhaustion. After the marathon is over, you can't just stop, otherwise you would cramp and hurt your muscles. You have to continue to jog for a while so you can stretch out and cool your body down: it's the same way with motherhood. Before you become a mom, you should educate yourself on the life of a mother. Once you are in the journey, you have to continue to learn and adapt. After you have raised your children from birth through adulthood, you still continue to parent, and then you grandparent. What you do when you are exhausted and *"done"* is what makes your journey memorable and something that prepares you for the future. The process is molding you into the person you want to be. If you rush the process, you will lose out on crucial steps which build your understanding and your impact on your children's lives. Don't cheat yourself out of personal growth.

This is not all doom and gloom. I think when you are forced to wait, you become balanced. If you desire to enjoy being a mom who can learn to see the "little blue socks" moments, both you and your children will enjoy their childhood.

If you fall in love with your role as mother and the process you take to get there, you will discover what makes great moms truly great. A great mom instructs but does not criticize. She teaches independence, and doesn't foster dependency. A mom who apologizes for her mistakes by confessing when she's wrong, is a humble woman. The best mom is a mom who admits she is not perfect, but strives to get to a place of teach-ability. Choose to be a mom who is ever learning, and doesn't stop personal growth in her or her children. It is within every one of us to be great moms. Remember, it is a process that evolves. As you get better, you will find it easier to be "the best mom in the world" for your children.

Parent With The End In Mind

Parenting with the end in mind is crucial in understanding the age and stage of your children. In the early stages of life, children need you to guide them with strong leaderships skills. There may be lots of "no-no's" or "don't do that." That should pass as the children learn self-control and understand your expectations. As they get older, they will seek facial expressions and hear voice inflections for correction or praise. In the teen years, they should have the inward knowledge of what is expected and then perform to the standard that was created. Without any of these social cues, they may have some problems in correctly performing the things required of them in different scenarios.

This is theoretical because when the rubber meets the road, you have to mesh this information with your child's personality and your ability to really stick to what you say. Young children have desires of their own that often override the instructions that adults are stating. When children grow older, their personality may be such that voice inflections and facial expressions mean little other than, "Oh, Mom's upset about something again." As teens grow up, they should know what is expected, but because they are sorting out their place in the world, they rebel and exert their own will over your expectations. All I can say is be patient and continue to parent with the end in mind.

Parenting with the end in mind is a philosophy that acknowledges the stages of growth, but forces us, as parents, to remain steadfast on certain key issues that pertain to character and personal safety. When we teach our children how to resolve conflicts by themselves instead of always needing their Mom or Dad, we are teaching them a valuable life lesson and skill. We are empowering them, despite our urge to jump in and save the day every time. It teaches them to practice problem-solving and seek out successful solutions.

When you give your children chores to perform and they do it half heartedly, you have the duty to teach them how to do it. Once the standard is set, do not accept less, otherwise you are doing your child a disservice. Parenting with the end in mind relays the message that the quality of their work is important and not just checking the block that it was done. Sure, it is easier for me to go back and do it right, but what message am I sending to my children by doing what I asked them to do? I am telling them that poor quality is acceptable and I am OK with it, when I really am not. I am allowing them to become lazy individuals who will one day be lazy workers. If you went on your job and did substandard work, how long do you think you would continue to be employed? Point made!

When children ask questions about religion or God, teach them by modeling and exposing them to the environment of religion and a personal relationship with God. When they question what they learned in areas, be sure to teach them to respect others. Correct the wrong thinking and teach them the correct response. Our goal is never to stop instructing, but to change the method of our teaching to build the child's character.

Teach younger children to take care of others' and their own personal property: this teaches them respect for themselves and for others. We don't allow our children to willfully break toys, carelessly cut up their clothing, or litter in public spaces. Respect for oneself and for others is a lifelong character trait that needs to be enforced. Don't allow your children to have continual indiscretions because it sends them a mixed message that respect is OK only sometimes.

For teens and young adults, diligence is a trait that has to be taught and reinforced. It's easily applied to schoolwork and chores. If a child is having a problem in school with a teacher and this is a challenging academic area for your child, do not be surprised, and don't immediately jump on the child's side. As mothers, we want to be mama bears and protect our children from any perceived threats. This should be the case, but as our children grow older, we have to learn to temper that enthusiasm with a good dose of reality, truth and the big picture.

When my sister, Sierra, had problems with both math and the math teacher, she was quick to blame the teacher and the class. The truth was that she was frustrated. She didn't want to ask too many questions in class for fear of being teased. She and the math teacher did not get along well and she chose not to do the homework.

Because we parent with the end in mind, we didn't immediately blame the teacher or the class size. Our goal was to help Sierra do better in class and get better grades. We were open-minded when we scheduled a conference with the teacher. After much discussion, James decided to work with the teaching staff first, then with Sierra. My husband dedicated every night to tutoring her for about an hour.

Before James got home, we made sure Sierra had her homework. He reviewed with her what was taught that day in class then gave her a mini-test. If she said she didn't have any work, he would create work for her to do. He even went so far as to contact all of her teachers daily to let them know that we were their partners in helping them do their job by making sure Sierra did her work.

His persistence forced her to be diligent in the things that were difficult for her. Her grades went from solid C's and D's to all A's and B's. She ultimately made the dean's list for three of the four quarters. It was that kind of turn around that diligence and dedication produced. Sierra realized that with as much work as she had done to turn her grades around, James had done just as much work, to help her stay on course.

Friends and sleepovers are other areas that require special attention. As parents, James and I see a direct correlation between the effort our children give during the week with their ability to have fun during the weekend. If they had several days of poor behavior either at school or at home, they are not allowed to hang out at a friend's house during the weekend. We do this not to be mean, but to give our children an opportunity for improvement. We don't allow ourselves to be manipulated by which day of the week they choose to behave well. Once we see that they have made a certain effort, we then focus on other areas and relax our requirements on the things they have mastered (provided they maintain an acceptable level of behavior and effort).

The biggest part of parenting with the end in mind came when we envisioned our child 15-20 years in the future. Would we like the person who they were and would we want to be around them for extended periods of time? Were we creating spoiled monsters or well-adjusted human beings who are considerate, diligent, and a pleasure to be around? If our children's personalities were that of co-workers, would we enjoy working with them daily on a job or would we dread seeing them? What type of environment will our grandchildren be exposed to and what type of influence will our children have as parents? When our grandchildren visit, will we be relieved when it is time for them to go home or will we be sad when they depart?

These are all end-in-mind type questions. The end is really a different phase of parenting. If you are only parenting for the now, you are harming both yourself and the future of your children. Yes, it is easy to give them what they want or let them do what they want, but what foundation are you laying and what type of person are you creating?

Your child will be in a position to affect this world in the next 20 years. That is a daunting task for anyone, but is your child up for the challenge? Have you equipped them with a vision and taught them balance? Do your children respect themselves, others, and their surroundings? Can your children solve problems without you? Have you given your children freedom to have fun, while learning to play and share with others? Do your children understand being responsible with finances and budgeting? Have you shown them that mom is a woman first, a wife second and a mother third?

So much to teach, and although we initially have 18 years in which to do it, it goes by so quickly. Focus on the now. If you have not begun to teach your children, but you are determined to be steadfast, make the decision to begin today. Start by taking small steps toward the greater goal of parenting with the end in mind.

> *"Forewarned, forearmed; to be prepared is half the victory."*
>
> – Miguel de Cervantes Saavedra

NOTES:

CHAPTER 16

LIVE FOR TODAY

"He who deliberates fully before taking a step will spend his entire life on one leg."
— Chinese proverb

I felt a little sad typing this last chapter. After tremendous effort, I have finally completed the pages of this book. The baby that I have conceived in my heart and labored over for years is finally here. I look back and I am excited for having set a goal of writing a book that I not only would be proud of, but would enjoy reading myself. It were as if I was watching my baby grow up right before my eyes, and then all of a sudden, it was done. My end-in-mind parenting does not know how my work will be received or treated. Maybe it will be criticized, maybe embraced and loved. I have the hope and dream that it becomes a resource, and a fun book that will plant a seed of thought in the minds and hearts of every person who reads it.

As moms, we go through a similar process when we find out we are pregnant. We think about names and baby themes. We figure out the logistics of where the baby will sleep and who will throw the baby shower. As our baby grows, we wonder about schools and the type of friends the child will have. Before the child graduates high school we help them choose which college to attend. After graduation from college, we wonder when our child will marry and have children of their own. I don't know about you, but I had all these thoughts on day two of being pregnant. I kept getting caught up in, "What would happen if..."

Sometimes, I got caught up in teaching values so much that I forgot to enjoy life. I would be so concerned with making sure that the children learned how to be polite and obedient that I would suck the fun out of some activities. I had to learn to balance teaching with joy.

I remember when Victoria was born; I was so enamored with her that I would stare at her for hours. When she started walking, I envisioned her walking down the aisle on her wedding day. Instead of enjoying watching her playing dress up, I would get caught up in the future of who she would become and what she would accomplish.

When Jimmy was younger, he had such an incredibly infectious laugh (and still does). His laugh would make you happy and you'd want to just start laughing, too. I remember being in a dentist's office one day, and all was quiet until Jimmy let out one of his huge, guttural laughs. Everyone in the office stared. At first it was like they couldn't believe how loud my kid was. I tried to shush him because I was slightly embarrassed, but he kept chuckling because something was so amusing to him. I finally gave in and joined his laughter parade. Suddenly, everyone began smiling and laughing, too. I had to stop and allow him to enjoy whatever it was that made him so elated.

Since Ella is still young, just about anything she does is cute. However, she is known as my international greeter. No matter where she goes, she has to stop and say, "Hello" to anyone she sees. At first, I tried to curtail her friendliness because of stranger danger. However, I soon realized that her smile and "Hello" are a breath of fresh air to people who are sad or need to remember the meaning of happiness. She makes cashiers smile with glee and carry on conversations. She makes even the most stoic person want to laugh. I have learned to allow her love to melt the heart of anyone fortunate enough to cross her path.

In case you're thinking about what I said in the previous chapter on parenting with the end in mind, this is not contradictory, but rather it adds another dimension. Parenting with the end in mind helps to build character traits in your child, while living for today helps you enjoy your children through the process of learning.

There are teachable moments in everything. One year we were working on the concept of recognizing money. The children had the opportunity to earn money by exhibiting certain character traits they had been taught. I would reward the kids for great behavior at school, having a great attitude about doing their homework, helping one another do some task, and for showing general kindness towards others. As they accumulated money from these things, they would eventually be able to buy candy from me.

The second part of the lesson was on budgeting and being wise about spending. I became the store where they could buy candy and other treats. I enjoyed putting the treats in a plastic storage container and treating it like the old-time penny candy stores. They looked with their eyes wide as they figured out how much money they had and what they could buy. They made tough choices and learned to barter or save for a bigger item. I loved the interaction between them and enjoyed being a part of it.

Occasionally, I act silly, just because I can (remember our family performs random acts of silliness). I break out in a crazy dance in the middle of the grocery store (this doesn't happen often, just when a good song comes on). As I dance down the aisle, Victoria and Jimmy both look around to see if anyone is staring. Their fear of eternal embarrassment doesn't bother me. I walk right up to them with a straight face and dance around them. It breaks the tension and makes them laugh. I know they secretly enjoy it and wish they could do it as well. Ella is the only one who will join me, but I think that is because she's young and doesn't know any better. We'll see as she grows up. I hope she will never feel too embarrassed to dance with me or stop and have fun in the moment.

If you live for today, you won't feel like your children have grown up in the blink of an eye. Time seems to linger longer. I often go into the children's rooms while they sleep and marvel at our memories. I reminisce how just yesterday, each of them got their first tooth or took their first step. I remember them hurting themselves and showering them with kisses until the tears stopped flowing. I recall their first crush and the incessant talk of how much they liked that person and how cute they were. So many things to remember, that I can't forget to cherish the now.

For all the past memories and even the future thoughts, there is no better place to be than in the present moment. Victoria came home practicing for her school's recital. She sang the sweetest song and it was so innocent and cute. The first time she sang it, I was in the midst of checking homework and cooking (my *"laundry"*). I heard the excitement in her voice and then the disappointment she felt because I only half-heard her. I apologized for not giving her my full attention. I stopped everything I was doing so I could listen to and hear the words of her song. I enjoyed her performance and the look on her face of sheer accomplishment at having learned the entire song in one day.

Just the other day, Ella and I were standing in the kitchen. James passed by and turned on the music. Some upbeat song started playing. Ella quickly stopped everything she was doing and started shaking her hips, shoulders, and "boo-tay." It was so sporadic, it made me start laughing. I love her ability to be free knowing that she enjoys the moment and goes with the flow. Now, every moment is not full of sugar, spice, and everything nice, but every moment is an opportunity to enjoy something new and refreshing.

Take the time to enjoy your today. If you enjoy being a mom, your children will enjoy you and their childhood. They will have a host of memories to draw upon when they are parents. Why not be the best you can be? Be the best mom in the world, and do it with a vision and a purpose. Don't be afraid to create memories and slow down long enough to remember them. Don't let the raising of your children be common or fall short of the goal because of a lack of direction, dedication, or vision.

You were created to be an extraordinary woman who cares for herself, creates a loving marriage with your husband, and prepares your children for life through your example and teaching. Today, choose to be the best YOU that YOU can be!

> *"Don't judge each day by the harvest you reap, but by the seeds that you plant."*
> – Robert Louis Stevenson

NOTES:

CHAPTER 17

TIP TIME

"Map out your future – but do it in pencil. The road ahead is as long as you make it. Make it worth the trip."

– Jon Bon Jovi

In this section you will find helpful tips and resources that I, as well as hundreds of mothers have contributed to make our lives manageable. You will find websites and books that can make your life easier. Please test cleaning products on a small inconspicuous area that needs to be cleaned. For medical items, please consult a family physician if you have questions. Again, please use discretion and do your research if you have questions. I do not guarantee any of the suggestions will work for you. These tips and ideas have been compiled from hundreds of moms, but in the end, it is all based on personal opinions and not hard science.

WEBSITES

www.Kraftfoods.com
Great if you need to put something together from random ingredients, many meals take 30 minutes or less.

www.about.com, www.google.com, www.yahoo.com, www.findhow.com, www.ehow.com, www.bing.com
Answers to any and every topic, especially on how to do things yourself.

www.webmd.com
Medical resource guide for all things medically related.

www.couponcabin.com
Great printable on-line discounts for many different vendors.

www.ediets.com, www.sparkpeople.com and www.babyfit.com
Free site for weight loss tips, and member boards.
Free site for tracking everything baby. Excellent articles, references and member boards.

www.childrensplace.com
Great deals on children's clothing, especially when a sale is going on. Clothes are high-quality and minimal shrinkage. The end-of-season sale always has great deals.

www.realsimple.com
Great website with helpful tips on recipes, organizing the home, and other magazine-based tips.

www.mommie911.com
An "everything mom" site.

www.greatschools.com
Excellent place to research school systems, counties, or individual schools when moving to a new area or changing schools.

www.facebook.com
Great site to reconnect with friends and family.

www.everydaycheapskate.com
Free weekly e-mail on finances, debt-proof living, and other weekly topics.

www.mosthelpfulhints.com, www.stilltasty.com
Helpful hints on cleaning, food, gardening, health, or saving money. Excellent advice on how to keep foods fresher longer, and other great questions answered.

www.twopeasinabucket.com
Great site for scrap booking.

www.redenvelope.com, www.overstock.com
Great site for general gift-giving.

SHOPPING TIPS

1. **DIAPER CHAMP** by Baby Trend is the best thing since sliced bread. It uses regular garbage bags and minimizes the smell of diapers. Change the bag weekly for older children or when the little diapers fill up quickly.
2. Take a **shopping list** and stick to it.
3. **Cut coupons** and **price compare** BEFORE you go to the store. Even if you don't cut coupons, you can save quite a lot by price matching. See also www.couponcabin.com.
4. Read labels. Not all fat-free or wheat products are the best. Sometimes they have as much sugar, sodium, or fat as the "high-calorie" version, but with less taste. Also, if "wheat" is not the first ingredient listed, it has a low "whole wheat" value.
5. Use a **bulk shopping** (BJ's, Costco, Sam's Club) **membership card** for some items, not all. Some items are actually more expensive per unit than at the regular grocery store. However things like dairy, some fresh fruit and veggies are usually less expensive.
6. If you can, **buy organic**: fresh veggies, fruit, and grain-fed or free-range meats. Organic is mainly helpful for thin-skinned items where pesticides would harm the flavor and make-up (veggies and some fruit). Grain-fed and free-range meats offer a better taste, quality and fewer additives.

MEAL PLANNER

1. **PLAN MEALS** a week or even a month in advance. This cuts down on guesswork, eating out often and frequent trips to the grocery store. You can prepare meals in advance and freeze them. If you put each recipe on an index card or store it on your computer, you can rotate the meals throughout the month so you don't have to recreate them every month. Initially it takes some time to set up, but after that, it is a piece of cake.
2. **CROCK-POTS** are one of the best appliances ever created. You simply get out your ingredients, put them in the Crock-Pot, set the temperature (low usually needs 6-8hrs and high usually 4-5hrs) and dinner is ready with minimal effort or labor on your part. You can even freeze prepared meals,

then put them in the Crock-Pot and let them cook during the day. If you are going to be gone more than 6-7 hours but still want your meal ready when you get home, use a light timer to start when you want the appliance on and when you want it to go off. This may help with longer delays when necessary.
3. **FREEZING MEALS** is an effective food preparation method. When making a meal, make twice the amount needed so that you can freeze the uncooked portion for use later. Place individual servings into aluminum containers and top them with aluminum foil, then wrap them in plastic wrap (if desired, place them inside of a freezer bag labeled with item contents and date). When you need a meal and you're short on time, pull out your pre-assembled meal and bake. You can even set your oven timer for easier use.
4. **RE-PURPOSING MEAL ITEMS** – if you have leftovers, you can always re-purpose them into a different meal. With Thanksgiving turkey, simply chop it up with fresh or frozen vegetables, mix it together with a little bit of cheese, rice or noodles, and make a pot pie.

PACKING FOR TRIPS

A few days before leaving (if possible), **figure out what you want to take.** If you can, iron, and hang all clothing for the trip. The night before, pull the hung and ironed clothes out of the closet and fold them in half. Place them directly in the suitcase with the hangers attached. When you get to your destination, pull the clothes directly out of the suitcase. Clothes should be relatively wrinkle-free and ready to wear. It also makes it easier for everyone if, when you hang the clothing, hang them as complete outfits so all everyone has to do is pull out the hanger and they are dressed for the day. This also works great for children during the school year.

LAUNDRY & CLEANING HELPERS

1. **Folex Carpet Cleaner** for cleaning carpets.
2. **Murphy's Oil Soap** is wonderful for cleaning all wood (whether 100 year old furniture or newly laid wood floors).

Laundry Can Wait

3. **Brown Paper Bag** takes melted candle wax out of carpet. Place a brown paper bag over the wax and place the iron on medium-heat setting over the bag. The bag should pick up the candle wax from the carpet.
4. When **folding laundry**, make it a family affair. Everyone folds, sorts, piles and then puts away the laundry.
5. When **folding sheets**, fold the flat sheet lengthwise into one piece, then fold lengthwise and put the fitted sheet on top. Fold lengthwise and put one of the pillowcases on top of the pile. Fold the sheet set onto itself and then tuck the entire sheet set into the 2nd pillowcase, and put it away. This can also be done with **towel sets** (towels, hand towels, and wash cloths). This eliminates the need to look for sets when making beds or restocking the bathroom towels.
6. **Purchasing inexpensive coffee** controls noxious odors. Put a few tablespoons of coffee into a filter or plastic container. Place the filter or container with coffee near the odor and allow it to sit for a few hours or until the noxious smell is gone. This can also work with **vinegar**. Pour ¼ cup vinegar into a bowl and allow the vinegar to evaporate. The smell should be gone when the vinegar is gone. If not, repeat with more vinegar.

MEMORY SAVERS

1. **Write it down** either on an electronic or traditional paper location.
2. <u>Computers</u>: **buy an external hard drive** and back up any sensitive or important information. This will safeguard against loss in case your computer crashes or you have a power surge. **Buy a surge-protector** for computer to prevent complete loss of information during power surges in the electricity.
3. **Digital Recorders**: most cellular phones have this feature, so check it out on your phone. You can also buy a traditional digital recorder or MP3 player to record notes to yourself or things to do.
4. **Scrapbook photos**: buy paper that is acid and lignin-free. Instead of letting all those wonderful memories pile up on the digital camera or hard drive, send them to a digital photo

website, and have them physically printed out. When you get the photos, place them in a scrapbook with a description of who is in the picture, when and where the picture was taken.
5. Collect all loose important papers on a board or get a **storage caddy**. If your refrigerator is a haven for pictures, notes, and other paper, get a ½" **3-ring binder with plastic sleeves** and place those items in the binder. This will eliminate clutter and keeps track of all necessary information. To affix the binder to the refrigerator, get double-sided sticky tape or even Velcro sticky pieces and place a couple on the back of the binder and the other piece on the refrigerator.

MEDICAL HELPS

1. **Constipation in infants:** If an infant is experiencing constipation, take a small pea-sized dab of castor oil and rub it on the baby's feet and tummy at night. The baby should have a bowel movement within 24-36 hours or less. DO NOT give the baby castor oil orally or mix any other laxative into baby's food without physician approval and direction.
2. **Nasal Congestion:** Use saline with aloe nasal spray for nose congestion or postnasal drip.
3. **Bee Stings:** For non-allergic bee stings, use a paste of baking soda and water to remove the stinger and the pain.
4. **Tick Removal:** apply a glob of liquid soap to a cotton ball. Cover the tick with the soap-soaked cotton ball and swab it for 15-20 seconds. The tick should come out and be stuck to the cotton ball when you lift it away.
5. **Burns:** If you get burned (sun or minor burns), apply a cold compress or put the burned area under cool running water. Let the compress sit for about 5-10 minutes then remove. If the area still hurts, reapply the cool compress. As long as you have pain, you should apply the compress. Once the pain subsides, you have helped the body to heal itself. If a more serious burn exists, seek medical attention. Never put oil, butter, or other warm substances on a burn as it causes the burn to "cook" and get worse.[12]
6. **Hiccups:** Eat a spoonful of sugar (dry) without water. You can drink water or other liquid after the hiccups have stopped.[13]

HELPFUL BOOKS

"*What to Expect When You're Expecting*" 4th – Heidi Murkoff and Sharon Mazel. Workman Publishing Company; 4th edition April 10, 2008.

"*The Baby Book: Everything You Need to Know About Your Baby from Birth to Age Two*" – William Sears, Martha Sears, Robert Sears, and James Sears. Little, Brown and Company; Revised edition (March 2003).

"*Your Pregnancy Week by Week*" – Glade B. Curtis and Judith Schuler. De Capo Press; 6 Rev Upd edition (December 3, 2007).

"*The Seven Minute Difference: Small Steps to Big Changes*" – Allyson Lewis. Kaplan Business (May 1, 2006).

"*The Happiest Baby on the Block*" – Harvey Karp. Bantam (May 27, 2003).

"*Baby Wise*" – Gary Ezzo and Robert Bucknam; Parent-Wise Solutions, Inc.; 4th edition (September 25, 2006).

"*The Five Love Languages: How to Express Heartfelt Commitment to Your Mate*" – Gary Chapman. Northfield Publishing (June 1, 1995).

"*His Needs, Her Needs: Building an Affair-Proof Marriage*" Willard F. Harley, Jr.Revell: 15th Anniversary Edition (April 1, 2001).

"*Every Woman's Guide To Looking & Feeling Sexy: From Head to Toe*" – Lisa Clinkscale Porter: JoMor Publishers; 1st edition (December 13, 2005).

"*Making Your Marriage A Love Story*" – C. Thomas & Maureen Anderson, Don Enevoldson; Winword Publishing; January 2005

> "*A good plan today is better than a perfect plan tomorrow.*"
>
> – General George S. Patton

THANK YOU

I want to personally thank you for taking time out of your lives to read this book. My intention is to raise self-awareness in the balance, understanding, and joy of being a woman, wife and mother. It is my wish that you be encouraged to plan a dream or vision for your life as a mom. I am hoping that you share this book with someone else and allow the information to start a groundswell of support.

I believe in this project and know that if enough women get their hands on it and add it to their arsenal of knowledge, it will cause many of us to do things differently or become more aware of who we are and our purpose.

When you purchase your copy, pick one up for a friend or two. If you buy multiple copies during one transaction, I will be more than happy to offer you a discount for your patronage. See the website for more specific details on discount rates.

I am available for speaking engagements to small and large groups of all types and will give your group a fundraiser's discount for each purchased item. Please contact me for more details.

Again, thank you for your support and please help me spread the word that *Laundry Can Wait!*

Endnotes

1. Lucille Ball, comedian, actress
2. www.reliableplant.com/article.asp?articleid=8259 issue 9/2007, Author: Douglas Vermeeren
3. *"The Seven Minute Difference: Small Steps to Big Changes"* – Allyson Lewis. Kaplan Business (May 1, 2006).
4. The Five Love Languages of Children by Gary Chapman & Ross Campbell. June 1, 1997 Northfield Publishing. 1st edition.
5. What to Expect When You're Expecting – Heidi Murkoff and Sharon Mazel. Workman Publishing Company; 4th Edition (April 10, 2008).
6. The Baby Book: Everything You Need to Know About Your Baby from Birth to Age Two – William & Martha Sears, Robert Sears, James Sears. Little, Brown and Company: Revised Edition (March 2003).
7. "Can't Control the Wind" – Ricky Skaggs, Bill Anderson, Roger Pirtle, Pat Lovely: '95 Mr. Bubba Music
8. King James Version of the Bible, Proverbs 22:6
9. King James Version of the Bible, Proverbs 22:15
10. "A Reason, A Season, A Lifetime" poem by Charlsy Soccer Chick: September 16, 1994.
11. "His Needs, Her Needs: Building an Affair-Proof Marriage" Williard F. Harley, Jr.: Revell; 15th Anniversary Edition. April 1, 2001.
12. Hint derived from www.mosthelpfulhints.com
13. Hint derived from www.mosthelpfulhints.com

LaVergne, TN USA
24 May 2010
183835LV00005B/7/P